Installing and Configuring Windows Server® 2012 Exam 70-410

Lab Manual

Craig Zacker

WILEY

EXECUTIVE EDITOR	John Kane
EDITORIAL ASSISTANT	Allison Winkle
DIRECTOR OF SALES	Mitchell Beaton
EXECUTIVE MARKETING MANAGER	Chris Ruel
SENIOR PRODUCTION & MANUFACTURING MANAGER	Janis Soo
PRODUCTION EDITOR	Eugenia Lee

www.wiley.com/college/microsoft

or

call the MOAC Toll-Free Number: 888-764-7001 (U.S. & Canada only)

ISBN 978-1-118-51158-9

Printed in the United States of America

10 9 8 7 6 5 4 3 2

BRIEF CONTENTS

CONTENTS

LAB 1
INSTALLING SERVERS

THIS LAB CONTAINS THE FOLLOWING EXERCISES AND ACTIVITIES:

Exercise 1.1   Performing a Clean Installation

Exercise 1.2   Performing an Upgrade Installation

Exercise 1.3   Installing Windows Server Migration Tools (WSMT)

Lab Challenge   Accessing a WSMT Distribution Point

BEFORE YOU BEGIN

The lab environment consists of computers connected to a local area network. The computers required for this lab are listed in Table 1-1.

Table 1-1
Computers Required for Lab 1

Computer	Operating System	Computer Name
New server	Bare metal	SVR-SO-A
Server for upgrade	Windows Server 2008 R2	SVR-SO-B
Server for migration	Windows Server 2008 R2	SVR-SO-C

In addition to the computers, you also require the software listed in Table 1-2 to complete Lab 1.

Table 1-2
Software Required for Lab 1

Software	Location
Installation disk for Windows Server 2012	Mounted on SVR-SO-A
Installation disk for Windows Server 2012	Mounted on SVR-SO-B
Lab 1 student worksheet	Lab01_worksheet.docx (provided by instructor)

Working with Lab Worksheets

Each lab in this manual requires that you answer questions, create screen shots, and perform other activities that you will document in a worksheet named for the lab, such as Lab01_worksheet.docx. It is recommended that you use a USB flash drive to store your worksheets, so you can submit them to your instructor for review. As you perform the exercises in each lab, open the appropriate worksheet file, fill in the required information, and save the file to your flash drive.

After completing this lab, you will be able to:

- Perform a clean Windows Server 2012 installation on a bare metal computer

- Upgrade a server to Windows Server 2012

- Install the Windows Server Migration Tools

Estimated lab time: 60 minutes

Exercise 1.1	Performing a Clean Installation
Overview	In this exercise, you install Windows Server 2012 on a new computer with no previously installed operating system.
Mindset	In many cases, organizations purchase servers without operating systems installed—sometimes called *bare metal servers*—either because they have an existing license agreement or because they intend to purchase the OS through another channel. In these cases, you perform what is known as a *clean operating system installation*, which is a procedure that creates a new server with its default operating system settings.
Completion time	10 minutes

1. Select the SVR-SO-A computer, on which the Windows Server 2012 installation disk is mounted and loaded. The Windows Setup page appears.

2. Click Next to accept the default values for the *Language to install, Time and currency format*, and *Keyboard or input method* parameters. Another Windows Setup page appears.

3. Click the *Install now* button. The *Select the operating system you want to install* page appears.

4. Select Windows Server 2012 Datacenter (Server with a GUI) and click Next. The *License terms* page appears.

5. Select *I accept the license terms* and click Next. The *Which type of installation do you want?* page appears.

6. Click Custom: Install Windows only (advanced). The *Where do you want to install Windows?* page appears (see Figure 1-1).

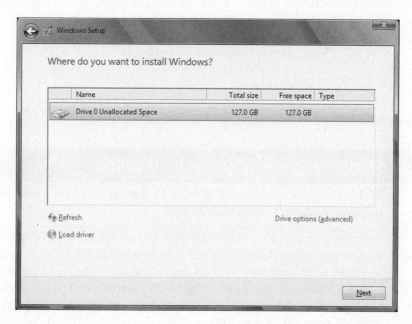

Figure 1-1
The *Where do you want to install Windows?* page

7. Select *Drive 0 Unallocated Space* and click Next. The *Installing Windows* page appears as the system installs Windows Server 2012.

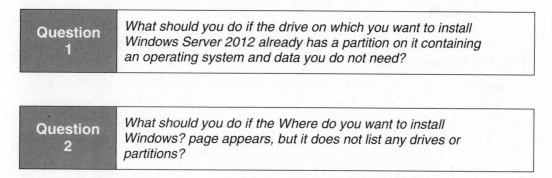

Question 1	What should you do if the drive on which you want to install Windows Server 2012 already has a partition on it containing an operating system and data you do not need?

Question 2	What should you do if the Where do you want to install Windows? page appears, but it does not list any drives or partitions?

8. After several minutes and a system restart, the Settings page appears.

9. In the *Password* and *Reenter password* text boxes, type **Pa$$w0rd** and click Finish. The Windows security page appears, showing the time.

10. Press Ctrl+Alt+Del and log on using the **Administrator** account with the password **Pa$$w0rd**. The Server Manager console appears.

11. Click Local Server in left pane, then click the Computer Name link. The System Properties sheet appears.

12. Click Change. The Computer Name/Domain Changes dialog box appears.

13. In the Computer name text box, type **SVR-SO-A** and click OK. A message box appears, telling you to restart the computer.

14. Click OK. Then click Close. Another message box appears.

15. Click Restart Now. The system restarts.

End of exercise. You can leave the windows open for the next exercise.

Exercise 1.2	Performing an Upgrade Installation
Overview	In this exercise, you install Windows Server 2012 on a computer running Windows Server 2008 R2.
Mindset	Assuming that a server meets all the requirements and has compatible drivers and applications installed, it is possible to perform an in-place upgrade, which retains all the system's software, data, and configuration settings. However, the more complex the server configuration, the more likely it will be for incompatibilities to arise, resulting in an end result that is unstable or otherwise problematic.
Completion time	20 minutes

1. Log on to the SVR-SO-B computer using the domain Administrator account and the password **Pa$$w0rd**, which loads Windows Server 2008 R2 and displays the Server Manager console.

2. Using Server Manager, determine which roles are installed on the server and make a note of them in the space on your worksheet.

3. Click Start > Run. The Run dialog box appears.

4. In the Open text box, type **d:\setup.exe** and click OK. The Windows Setup window for Windows Server 2012 appears.

5. Click Install Now. The *Get important updates for Windows Setup* page appears.

6. Click No thanks. The *Select the operating system you want to install* page appears.

7. Select Windows Server 2012 Datacenter (Server with a GUI) and click Next. The *License terms* page appears.

8. Select *I accept the license terms* and click Next. The *Which type of installation do you want?* page appears.

9. Click *Upgrade: Install Windows and keep files, settings, and applications*. The compatibility report page appears.

Question 3	Under what conditions would the Upgrade option not be available to you during the Windows Server 2012 installation process.

10. Review the compatibility information provided and click Next. The Upgrading Windows page appears.

Question 4	The compatibility notes that appear during this exercise are recommendations; they do not prevent you from performing the upgrade. However, in a real-world upgrade situation, this might not be the case. Give an example of a compatibility note that will stop the upgrade process and force you to take action before restarting the installation.

11. The upgrade process installs Windows Server 2012 and any compatible applications that existed on the server before you began the upgrade. The computer restarts several times and ends up on the main logon screen.

NOTE	The length of time required for the Windows Server 2012 upgrade process can be 20 minutes or more, depending on the number and type of applications, files, and configuration settings on the computer at the outset.

12. Press Ctrl+Alt+Del and log on using the **Administrator** account and the password **Pa$$w0rd**. The Windows Server 2012 desktop appears and Server Manager loads.

13. Click Local Server in the left pane, take a screen shot of the Properties window by pressing Alt+Prt Scr, and then paste it into your Lab 1worksheet file in the page provided by pressing Ctrl+V.

14. Using Server Manager, determine which roles are installed on the server and make a note of them in the space on your worksheet.

Question 5	What proof do you have that the procedure just completed has upgraded the operating system on the computer and not just performed a new, clean installation?

End of exercise. You can leave the windows open for the next exercise.

Exercise 1.3	Installing Windows Server Migration Tools
Overview	In this exercise, you install the Windows Server Migration Tools, which enable you to migrate roles from an existing server to a new server running Windows Server 2012.
Mindset	Compared to an in-place upgrade, a side-to-side migration is a more complex procedure, but usually results in a more stable server configuration. Windows Server 2012 includes tools that facilitate the migration of certain roles, but before you can use them, you must deploy those tools on both the source and the destination server.
Completion time	10 minutes

1. Select the SVR-SO-A computer, on which you installed Windows Server 2012, previously in this lab. SVR-SO-A will be the destination server in the migration.

2. Press Ctrl+Alt+Del. The Windows login page appears, with the Administrator user account.

3. In the Password text box, type **Pa$$w0rd** and press Enter. The Server Manager console loads.

4. In Server Manager, click *Manage > Add Roles and Features*. The Add Roles and Features Wizard appears, displaying the *Before you begin* page.

5. Click Next. The *Select installation type* page appears.

6. Click Next to accept the default *Role-based or feature-based installation* type. The *Select destination server* page appears.

7. Click Next to accept the default settings, which install the selected roles and features to the local server. The *Select server roles* page appears.

8. Click Next to continue. The *Select features* page appears (see Figure 1-2).

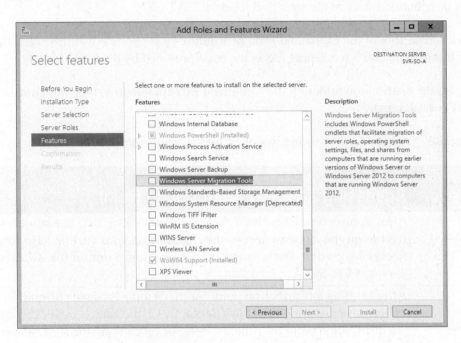

Figure 1-2
The *Select features* page of the Add Roles and Features Wizard

9. Select the Windows Server Migration Tools check box and click Next. The *Confirm installation selections* page appears.

10. Click Install. The wizard installs the Windows Server Migration Tools feature.

11. When the installation is completed, click Close. The wizard closes.

12. To install the Windows Server Migration Tools on SVR-SO-C, the source server in the migration, you must create a distribution folder on SVR-SO-A and populate it with the installation files for the tools. To create a distribution folder for the Windows Server Migration Tools on SVR-SO-A, open the Start screen and right-click anywhere around the border to display the icon bar.

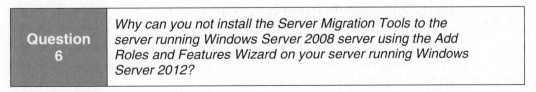

| Question 6 | Why can you not install the Server Migration Tools to the server running Windows Server 2008 server using the Add Roles and Features Wizard on your server running Windows Server 2012? |

13. Click All apps. The Apps page appears.

14. Right-click Command Prompt and, from the icon bar, select Run as administrator. An Administrator: Command Prompt window appears.

15. At the prompt, type **cd \windows\system32\ServerMigrationTools** and press Enter.

16. At the prompt, type **SmigDeploy.exe/package/architecture "amd64" /os WS08R2/ path "C:\users"** and press Enter. The program creates the Windows Server Deployment Tools distribution folder in the specified location.

17. Take a screen shot of the Command Prompt window by pressing Alt+Prt Scr and then paste it into your Lab 1 worksheet file in the page provided by pressing Ctrl+V.

18. To share the distribution folder, in the Command Prompt window, type **net share WSMT=C:\Users.**

End of exercise. You can leave the windows open for the next exercise.

Lab Challenge	Accessing a WSMT Distribution Point
Overview	After completing Exercise 1.3, a user on SVR-SO-C, the source server for the migration, can access the installation files for the Windows Server Migration Tools from the distribution point on the destination server, SVR-SO-A.
Mindset	After creating a distribution point for the Windows Server Migration Tools on the server running Windows Server 2012, the source server can access the distribution point over the network, or by copying the files on a portable storage device.
Completion time	10 minutes

To complete the challenge, you must install the Windows Server Migration Tools on SVR-SO-C by accessing the shared distribution folder on SVR-SO-A and running the Smigdeploy.exe program with no parameters from an Administrative command prompt. Then, take a screen shot of the Command Prompt window by pressing Alt+Prt Scr and then paste it into your Lab 1worksheet file in the page provided by pressing Ctrl+V.

HINT	*The distribution folder is already shared on SVR-SO-A, but before SVR-SO-C can access the share, you must turn on File and Printer Sharing on SVR-SO-A.*

End of lab.

LAB 2
CONFIGURING SERVERS

THIS LAB CONTAINS THE FOLLOWING EXERCISES AND ACTIVITIES:

Exercise 2.1   Completing Post-Installation Tasks

Exercise 2.2   Adding Roles and Features

Exercise 2.3   Converting the GUI Interface to Server Core

Lab Challenge   Using the Server Core Interface

BEFORE YOU BEGIN

The lab environment consists of computers connected to a local area network, along with a server that functions as the domain controller for a domain called *adatum.com*. The computers required for this lab are listed in Table 2-1.

Table 2-1
Computers Required for Lab 2

Computer	Operating System	Computer Name
Domain controller	Windows Server 2012	SVR-DC-A
New member server	Windows Server 2012	SVR-MBR-B

In addition to the computers, you also require the software listed in Table 2-2 to complete Lab 2.

Table 2-2
Software Required for Lab 2

Software	Location
Lab 2 student worksheet	Lab02_worksheet.docx (provided by instructor)

Working with Lab Worksheets

Each lab in this manual requires that you answer questions, create screen shots, and perform other activities that you will document in a worksheet named for the lab, such as Lab02_worksheet.docx. It is recommended that you use a USB flash drive to store your worksheets, so you can submit them to your instructor for review. As you perform the exercises in each lab, open the appropriate worksheet file, fill in the required information, and save the file to your flash drive.

After completing this lab, you will be able to:

- Complete the initial setup tasks required on a newly installed server

- Convert a Windows Server 2012 interface from GUI to Server Core and back again

- Add roles and features using the wizard and Windows PowerShell

Estimated lab time: 50 minutes

Exercise 2.1	Completing Post-Installation Tasks
Overview	In this exercise, you complete the tasks necessary to set up a server on which Windows Server 2012 has just been installed.
Mindset	When you purchase a server from an original equipment manufacturer (OEM) with Windows Server 2012 installed, the factory runs a program called *Sysprep.exe* that prepares the server for distribution by erasing all the user-specific information on the system.
Completion time	20 minutes

1. Select the SVR-MBR-B computer, on which Windows Server 2012 has just been installed. The Settings page appears, displaying the server's license terms.

2. Select the *I accept the license terms for using Windows* check box and click Accept. The Region and Language page appears.

3. Click Next to accept the default values for the *Country and Region, Language*, and *Keyboard Layout* parameters. Another Settings page appears.

4. In the *Password* and *Reenter password* text boxes, type **Pa$$w0rd** and click Finish. The Windows security page appears, showing the time.

5. Press Ctrl+Alt+Delete and, in the Password text box, type **Pa$$w0rd** and click the right arrow. The system logs on the Administrator user and the Server Manager console appears.

6. In the left pane, click Local Server. The Properties tile appears in the right pane.

7. Click the Time Zone value. The Date and Time dialog box appears (see Figure 2-1).

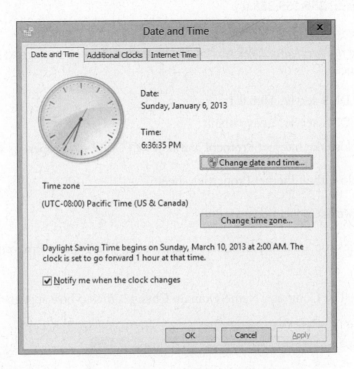

Figure 2-1
The Date and Time dialog box

8. Click Change Time Zone, if necessary. The Time Zone Settings dialog box appears.

9. In the Time Zone drop-down list, select the *(UTC -05:00) Eastern Time (US & Canada)* time zone and click OK.

Question 1	*Why must you set the time zone to Eastern time, even if that is not where you are currently located?*

10. Click OK to close the Date and Time dialog box.

11. Click the Ethernet value. The Network Connections dialog box appears.

12. Right-click the Ethernet connection and, from the context menu, select Properties. The Ethernet Properties sheet appears.

13. Double-click Internet Protocol Version 4 (TCP/IPv4). The Internet Protocol Version 4 (TCP/IPv4) Properties sheet appears.

14. Select the *Use the following IP address* option and, in the text boxes, type the following values:

   - IP address: **10.0.0.2**
   - Subnet mask: **255.255.255.0**
   - Default gateway: Leave blank

15. Select the *Use the following DNS server addresses* option and, in the text boxes, type the following values:

   - Preferred DNS server: **10.0.0.1**
   - Alternate DNS server: Leave blank

16. Click OK to close the Internet Protocol Version 4 (TCP/IPv4) Properties sheet.

17. Click OK to close the Ethernet Properties sheet.

18. Close the Network Connections window.

19. In the Properties tile, click the *Computer name* value. The System Properties sheet appears.

20. Click Change. The Computer Name/Domain Changes dialog box appears (see Figure 2-2).

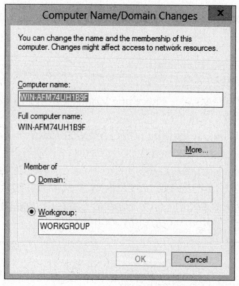

Figure 2-2
The Computer Name/Domain Changes dialog box

21. In the Computer name text box, type **SVR-MBR-B**.

22. Select the Domain option and, in the Domain text box, type **adatum.com** and click OK. The Windows Security dialog box appears.

23. In the User name text box, type **Administrator**.

24. In the Password text box, type **Pa$$w0rd** and click OK. A *Welcome to the adatum.com* message box appears.

25. Click OK. A message box appears, prompting you to restart the computer.

26. Click OK.

27. Click Close to close the System Properties dialog box. Another message box appears, prompting you to restart the computer.

28. Click Restart now. The system restarts.

29. Log on to the system using the **Administrator** account and the password **Pa$$w0rd**. When Server Manager opens, click Local Server in the left pane, take a screen shot of the Properties window by pressing Alt+Prt Scr, and then paste it into your Lab 2 worksheet file in the page provided by pressing Ctrl+V. Your screen shot should show the parameters you modified during this exercise.

End of exercise. You can leave the windows open for the next exercise.

Exercise 2.2	Adding Roles and Features
Overview	In this exercise, you use the Add Roles and Features Wizard to install additional components to a server running Windows Server 2012.
Mindset	One of the most basic tasks that administrators perform when setting up a server is to install the roles and features providing the software the server needs to perform its basic functions.
Completion time	10 minutes

1. On the SVR-MBR-B computer, which has the Server Manager console open, select Manage > Add Roles and Features. The Add Roles and Features Wizard appears, displaying the *Before you begin* page.

2. Click Next. The *Select Installation Type* page appears.

3. Leave the *Role-based or feature-based installation* radio button selected and click Next. The *Select Destination Server* page appears.

Question 2	How can you install these same roles and features on SVR-MBR-B by using tools on the SVR-DC-A server?

4. Click Next to accept the default local server. The *Select Server Roles* page appears.

5. Select the Print and Document Services check box. The *Add features that are required for Print and Document Services?* page appears.

6. Click Add features.

7. Select the Web Server (IIS) check box. The *Add features that are required for Web Server (IIS)?* page appears.

8. Click Add features.

9. Click Next. The *Select features* page appears. Select the following check boxes:

   - Group Policy Management

   - Internet Printing Client

   - Windows Server Backup

10. Click Next. The *Print and Document Services* page appears.

11. Click Next. The *Select role services* page appears.

12. Click Next. The *Web Server Role (IIS)* page appears.

13. Click Next. The *Select role services* page appears.

14. Click Next. The *Confirm installation selections* page appears.

15. Click Install. The wizard installs the selected roles and features.

16. Click Close.

Question 3	How would the installation of the roles and features selected in this exercise differ if the server was running Windows Server 2008 R2?

Question 4	How can you prove that the Web Server (IIS) role is installed on the server?

End of exercise. You can leave the windows open for the next exercise.

Exercise 2.3	Converting the GUI Interface to Server Core
Overview	Windows Server 2012, for the first time, enables you to convert a server installed using the full graphical user interface to one that uses Server Core. This enables administrators who are less familiar with the Windows PowerShell interface to install and configure a server using the familiar GUI tools, and then convert it to Server Core to minimize hardware resource utilization.
Mindset	What advantages does Server Core provide over the full Windows Server 2012 interface?
Completion time	10 minutes

1. On the SVR-MBR-B computer, which has the Server Manager console open, select Manage > Remove Roles and Features. The Remove Roles and Features Wizard appears, displaying the *Before you begin* page.

2. Click Next. The *Select destination server* page appears.

3. Click Next to select the local server. The *Remove Server Roles* page appears.

4. Click Next. The *Remove features* page appears.

5. Scroll down in the list and expand the User Interfaces and Infrastructure feature (see Figure 2-3).

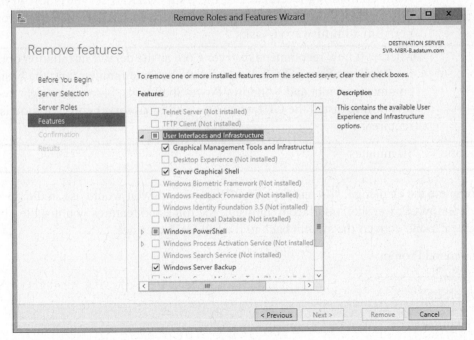

Figure 2-3
The Remove features page

6. Clear the check boxes for the following component:

   • Graphical Management Tools and Infrastructure

7. The Remove features that require Graphical Management Tools and Infrastructure dialog box appears.

8. Click Remove Features. Confirm that the Server Graphical Shell checkbox was also cleared.

9. Click Next. The Confirm removal selections page appears.

10. Select the *Restart the destination server automatically if required* check box and then confirm the selection with Yes. Click Remove. The Removal progress page appears as the wizard uninstalls the feature.

11. Click Close. When the removal is completed, the computer restarts.

12. Log on to the system using the **Administrator** account and the password **Pa$$w0rd.**

13. Take a screen shot of the Server Core interface by pressing Alt+Prt Scr and then paste it into your Lab 2 worksheet file in the page provided by pressing Ctrl+V.

End of exercise. You can leave the windows open for the next exercise.

Lab Challenge	Using the Server Core Interface
Overview	After completing Exercise 2.3, the SVR-MBR-B server is left in the Server Core interface. Users must work from the command line to perform administrative tasks.
Mindset	Microsoft now recommends Server Core as the default installation option for Windows Server 2012. Users should become familiar with the basic command prompt and Windows PowerShell tools, because it might not be practical to install the GUI whenever additional server configuration is required.
Completion time	10 minutes

To complete the challenge, you must specify the commands you would use in the Server Core Windows PowerShell interface to uninstall the roles and features you installed in Exercise 2.2 and convert the system back to the full GUI interface.

In Command Prompt:

_____

In PowerShell:

_____

End of lab.

LAB 3
CONFIGURING LOCAL STORAGE

THIS LAB CONTAINS THE FOLLOWING EXERCISES AND ACTIVITIES:

Exercise 3.1   Initializing Disks

Exercise 3.2   Creating Simple Volumes

Exercise 3.3   Creating a Storage Pool

Lab Challenge   Removing Storage Components

BEFORE YOU BEGIN

The lab environment consists of computers connected to a local area network, along with a server that functions as the domain controller for a domain called *adatum.com*. The computers required for this lab are listed in Table 3-1.

Table 3-1
Computers Required for Lab 3

Computer	*Operating System*	*Computer Name*
Domain controller	Windows Server 2012	SVR-DC-A
Member server	Windows Server 2012	SVR-MBR-B
Member server with three additional SCSI hard drives	Windows Server 2012	SVR-MBR-C

In addition to the computers, you also require the software listed in Table 3-2 to complete Lab 3.

Table 3-2
Software Required for Lab 3

Software	Location
Lab 3 student worksheet	Lab03_worksheet.docx (provided by instructor)

Working with Lab Worksheets

Each lab in this manual requires that you answer questions, create screen shots, and perform other activities that you will document in a worksheet named for the lab, such as Lab03_worksheet.docx. It is recommended that you use a USB flash drive to store your worksheets, so you can submit them to your instructor for review. As you perform the exercises in each lab, open the appropriate worksheet file, fill in the required information, and save the file to your flash drive.

After completing this lab, you will be able to:

- Initialize new disks

- Create storage spaces, disks, and volumes with Server Manager

- Create volumes with the Disk Management snap-in

Estimated lab time: 60 minutes

Exercise 3.1	Initializing Disks
Overview	In this exercise, you use two different tools to bring three new disks online and initialize them in preparation for creating storage volumes.
Mindset	Adding disk drives is a common server hardware upgrade, requiring an administrator to prepare them for use.
Completion time	15 minutes

1. Log on to the SVR-MBR-C computer using the domain Administrator account and the password **Pa$$w0rd**. In Server Manager, click File and Storage Services. A File and Storage Services submenu appears (see Figure 3-1).

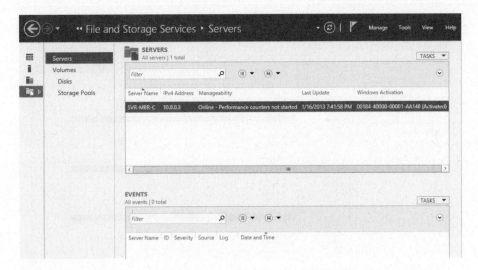

Figure 3-1
The File and Storage Services submenu in Server Manager

2. Click Disks. The Disks page appears, showing one online disk and three offline disks.

Question 1	The three offline disks all use the SCSI bus type, whereas the online disk uses the ATA bus. Why can't the three offline disks use the ATA bus as well?

3. Right-click the offline disk number 1 and, from the context menu, select Bring Online. A message box appears, warning you not to bring the disk online if it is already online and connected to another server.

4. Click Yes. The disk's status changes to Online.

5. Right-click the same offline disk number 1 and, from the context menu, select Initialize. A message box appears, warning you that any data on the disk will be erased.

6. Click Yes. The disk is partitioned and ready to create volumes.

7. In Server Manager, click Tools > Computer Management. The Computer Management console appears.

8. In the left pane, click Disk Management. The Disk Management snap-in appears (see Figure 3-2).

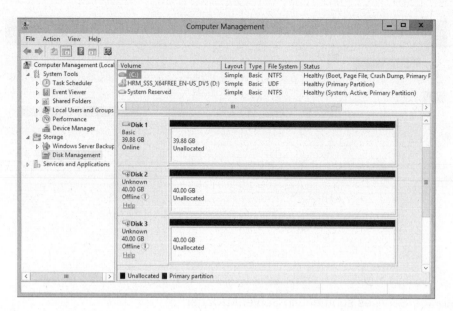

Figure 3-2
The Disk Management snap-in

9. Right-click the Disk 2 tile and, from the context menu, select Online.

10. Right-click the Disk 2 tile a second time and, from the context menu, select Initialize Disk. The Initialize Disk dialog box appears.

11. Select the GPT (GUID Partition Table) option and click OK. The Disk 2 status changes to Online.

12. Repeat steps 9 to 11 to initialize Disk 3.

End of exercise. You can leave the windows open for the next exercise.

Question 2	What advantage is there to using the Disk Management snap-in to initialize new disks, rather than Server Manager?

Exercise 3.2	Creating Simple Volumes
Overview	In this exercise, you use two methods to create simple volumes, using Server Manager and the Disk Management snap-in.
Mindset	Server Manager and Disk Management both provide wizards for creating simple volumes, with similar capabilities.
Completion time	15 minutes

1. On SVR-MBR-C, in Server Manager, in the File and Storage Services submenu, click Volumes. The Volumes home page appears.

2. Click Tasks > New Volume. The New Volume Wizard appears, displaying the *Before you begin* page.

3. Click Next. The *Select the server and disk* page appears.

4. Select Disk 1 and click Next. The *Specify the size of the volume* page appears.

5. In the *Volume size* text box, type **10** and click Next. The *Assign to a drive letter or folder* page appears.

6. Click Next. The *Select file system settings* page appears.

7. Click Next. The *Confirm selections* page appears.

8. Click Create. The *Completion* page appears.

9. Click Close. The new volume appears in the Volumes pane.

10. Switch to the Computer Management console. The new volume you just created appears in the Disk 1 pane of the Disk Management snap-in.

11. Right-click the unallocated space on Disk 2 and, from the context menu, select New Simple Volume. The New Simple Volume Wizard appears, displaying the *Welcome* page.

12. Click Next. The *Specify Volume Size* page appears.

13. In the *Simple volume size in MB* spin box, type **10000** and click Next. The *Assign Drive Letter or Path* page appears.

14. Click Next. The *Format Partition* page appears.

15. Click Next. The *Completing the New Simple Volume Wizard* page appears.

16. Click Finish. The wizard creates the volume, and it appears in the Disk 2 pane.

Question 3	*What Windows PowerShell commands should you use to create a simple volume of the same size on disk 3 using the drive letter G:?*

17. Create a 10 GB simple volume on disk 3 with the drive letter G: using Windows PowerShell.

18. Press Alt+Prt Scr to take a screen shot of the Disk Management snap-in, showing the three volumes you created, and then press Ctrl+V to paste the resulting image into the Lab 3 worksheet file in the page provided.

End of exercise. Close Computer Management before you begin the next exercise.

Exercise 3.3	Creating a Storage Pool
Overview	In this exercise, you use the Server Manager console to create a storage pool, which consists of space from multiple physical disks.
Mindset	Storage pools are a new feature in Windows Server 2012, which enable you to create a flexible storage subsystem with various types of fault tolerance.
Completion time	15 minutes

1. On SVR-MBR-C, in Server Manager, on the File and Storage Services submenu, click Storage Pools. The Storage Pools home page appears (see Figure 3-3).

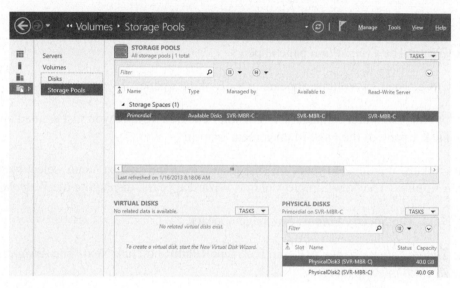

Figure 3-3
The Storage Pools home page

2. In the Storage Pools tile, click Tasks > New Storage Pool. The New Storage Pool Wizard appears, displaying the *Before you begin* page.

3. Click Next. The *Specify a storage pool name and subsystem* page appears.

4. In the Name text box, type **Pool1** and click Next. The *Select physical disks for the storage pool* page appears.

5. Select the check boxes for PhysicalDisk1 and PhysicalDisk2 in the list and click Next. The *Confirm selections* page appears.

6. Click Create. The wizard creates the storage pool.

7. Click Close. The new pool appears in the Storage Pools tile.

8. Select Pool1.

9. In the Virtual Disks tile, click Tasks > New Virtual Disk. The New Virtual Disk Wizard appears, displaying the *Before you begin* page.

10. Click Next. The *Select the storage pool* page appears.

11. Click Next. The *Specify the virtual disk name* page appears.

12. In the name text box, type **Data1** and click Next. The *Select the storage layout* page appears.

13. In the layout list, select Parity and click Next. A warning appears, stating that the storage pool does not contain a sufficient number of physical disks to support the Parity layout.

Question 4	Why can't the wizard create a virtual disk using the Parity layout when there are only two physical disks in the storage pool?

14. In the layout list, select Mirror and click Next. The *Specify the provisioning type* page appears.

15. Leave the default Fixed option selected and click Next. The *Specify the size of the virtual disk* page appears.

16. In the Virtual disk size text box, type **10** and click Next. The *Confirm selections* page appears.

17. Click Create. The wizard creates the virtual disk and the *View results* page appears. Deselect the *Create a volume when this wizard closes* option.

18. Click Close. The virtual disk appears on the Storage Pools page.

19. Press Alt+Prt Scr to take a screen shot of the Storage Pools page, showing the storage pool and the virtual disk you created, and then press Ctrl+V to paste the resulting image into the Lab 3 worksheet file in the page provided.

20. In the Virtual Disks tile, right-click the Data1 disk you just created and, from the context menu, select New Volume. The New Volume Wizard appears.

21. Using the wizard, create a volume on Disk 4 (Data1) using all of the available space, the NTFS file system, and the drive letter J:.

End of exercise. Close any open windows before you begin the next exercise.

Question 5	At this point in the lab, what would happen to any data stored on the E:, F:, G:, and J: drives if Disk 2 on the server was to fail?

Lab Challenge	Removing Storage Components
Overview	In addition to the graphical tools provided with Windows Server 2012, you can also manipulate the storage subsystem using Windows PowerShell commands.
Completion time	15 minutes

To complete this challenge, list the Windows PowerShell commands needed to delete all of the storage components you created during this lab on the SCSI disks of SVR-MBR-C. Then, restart SVR-MBR-C and take a screen shot of the Storage Pools page, showing the removal of the storage pool and the virtual disk you created. Press Ctrl+V to paste the resulting image into the Lab 3 worksheet file in the page provided.

End of lab.

LAB 4
CONFIGURING FILE AND SHARE ACCESS

THIS LAB CONTAINS THE FOLLOWING EXERCISES AND ACTIVITIES:

Exercise 4.1   Sharing a Folder

Exercise 4.2   Testing Share Access

Exercise 4.3   Working with NTFS Permissions

Exercise 4.4   Creating Shares with Server Manager

Lab Challenge   Creating Shares with Windows PowerShell

BEFORE YOU BEGIN

The lab environment consists of computers connected to a local area network, along with a server that functions as the domain controller for a domain called *adatum.com*. The computers required for this lab are listed in Table 4-1.

Table 4-1
Computers Required for Lab 4

Computer	Operating System	Computer Name
Domain controller	Windows Server 2012	SVR-DC-A
Member server	Windows Server 2012	SVR-MBR-B
Member server with three additional SCSI hard drives	Windows Server 2012	SVR-MBR-C

In addition to the computers, you also require the software listed in Table 4-2 to complete Lab 4.

Table 4-2
Software Required for Lab 4

Software	Location
Lab 4 student worksheet	Lab04_worksheet.docx (provided by instructor)

Working with Lab Worksheets

Each lab in this manual requires that you answer questions, create screen shots, and perform other activities that you will document in a worksheet named for the lab, such as Lab04_worksheet.docx. It is recommended that you use a USB flash drive to store your worksheets, so you can submit them to your instructor for review. As you perform the exercises in each lab, open the appropriate worksheet file, fill in the required information, and save the file to your flash drive.

After completing this lab, you will be able to:

- Share folders using File Explorer

- Share folders using Server Manager

- Configure share and NTFS permissions

Estimated lab time: 60 minutes

Exercise 4.1	Sharing a Folder
Overview	In this exercise, you create a folder share using the File Explorer interface.
Mindset	How familiar are you with the traditional tools for creating and managing shares?
Completion time	15 minutes

1. Log on to the SVR-MBR-C computer, using the domain Administrator account and the password **Pa$$w0rd**. Click the File Explorer icon on the taskbar. A File Explorer window appears.

2. In File Explorer, select the E: drive and create a new folder called **Accounting**.

3. In the navigation pane, select the Accounting folder you just created. Then, right-click anywhere in the contents pane and, from the context menu, select New > Rich Text Document. Give the file the name **Budget** and double-click it to open the file in WordPad.

4. Type some text in the file and close the WordPad window, saving the changes to the file when prompted to do so.

5. Right-click the Accounting folder you created and, from the context menu, select Properties. The Accounting Properties sheet appears.

6. Click the Sharing tab, and then click Advanced Sharing. The Advanced Sharing dialog box appears.

7. Select the Share This Folder check box.

8. In the Share Name text box, change the default value (Accounting) to **Spreadsheets**.

9. Click Permissions. The Permissions For Spreadsheets dialog box appears.

10. For the Everyone special identity, clear all check boxes in the Allow column.

11. Click Add. The Select Users or Groups dialog box appears.

12. In the Enter The Object Names To Select box, type **Domain Admins** and click OK (log in with Administrator/Pa$$w0rd if necessary). The Domain Admins group appears in the Group Or User Names list in the Permissions For Spreadsheets dialog box.

Question 1	What share permissions does a newly added group receive by default?

13. With the Domain Admins group highlighted, select the Full Control check box in the Allow column, which selects the Change check box as well. Click Apply.

14. Using the same procedure, add the Domain Users group to the Group Or User Names list, and assign it the Allow Read permission only.

15. Take a screen shot of the Permissions For Spreadsheets dialog box by pressing Alt+Prt Scr, and then paste the resulting image into the Lab 4 worksheet file in the page provided by pressing Ctrl+V.

16. Click OK to close the Permissions For Spreadsheets dialog box.

17. Click OK to close the Advanced Sharing dialog box.

18. Click Close to close the Accounting Properties sheet.

End of exercise. Close any open windows before you begin the next exercise.

Exercise 4.2	Testing Share Access
Overview	In this exercise, you demonstrate the use of share permissions to limit access to file system shares.
Mindset	What are the capabilities of share permissions, and do you as an administrator want to make use of them?
Completion time	15 minutes

1. On SVR-MBR-B, log on using the domain account **Student** with the password **Pa$$w0rd**.

2. On SVR-MBR-B, click the Windows PowerShell button in the taskbar. The Windows PowerShell window appears.

3. At the Windows PowerShell prompt, type **explorer \\svr-mbr-c\Spreadsheets** and press Enter. A File Explorer window appears, displaying the contents of the share you created in the previous exercise.

4. Double-click the Budget file to open it in WordPad.

5. Modify the text in the Budget file and click File > Save. A message box appears, stating that access to the file is denied.

6. Click OK and close WordPad without saving.

7. Try to delete the budget file. A File Access Denied message box appears.

8. Click Cancel.

Question 2	Why are you unable to modify or delete the Budget file?

9. Log off the SVR-MBR-B server and log on again, but this time use the domain **Administrator** account and the password **Pa$$w0rd**.

10. Try again to open the Budget file. Modify its contents, and save it.

Question 3	Why are you now able to modify the Budget file?

End of exercise. Close any open windows before you begin the next exercise.

Exercise 4.3	Working with NTFS Permissions
Overview	In this exercise, you demonstrate the use of NTFS permissions in combination with share permissions.
Mindset	The use of share permissions and NTFS permissions together can be confusing, especially when there are multiple administrators working on the same servers. Permissions should, therefore, be dictated by a company policy adhered to by everyone.
Completion time	15 minutes

·1. On SVR-MBR-C, in File Explorer, right-click the Accounting folder you created in Exercise 4.1 and, from the context menu, select Properties. The Accounting Properties sheet appears.

2. Click the Security tab (see Figure 4-1).

Figure 4-1
The Security tab of the Accounting Properties sheet

3. Click Edit. The Permissions For Accounting dialog box appears.

4. Click Add. The Select Users, Computers, Service Accounts, or Groups dialog box appears.

5. In the *Enter The Object Names To Select* text box, type **Student** and click OK. The Student user appears in the Group Or User Names list in the Permissions For Accounting dialog box.

Question 4	For the purposes of this lab, you assign permissions directly to the Student user account. How does this differ from standard enterprise networking practice?

6. Select the Student user and, in the Permissions for Student box, select the Allow Full Control check box and click OK.

7. Click OK again to close the Accounting Properties sheet.

8. On SVR-MBR-B, log on using the **Student** account and the password **Pa$$w0rd**.

9. Open the Run dialog box and, in the Open text box, type **\\svr-mbr-c\Spreadsheets** and click OK. A File Explorer window appears, displaying the contents of the share you created in Exercise 4.1.

10. Open the Budget file, modify the text, and try to save your changes. The system denies you access to the file.

Question 5	Why are you unable to modify the Budget file, when you have the Allow Full Control NTFS permission?

11. On SVR-MBR-C, log off of the system and then log on again using the **Student** account and the password **Pa$$w0rd**.

12. Open File Explorer, browse to the Accounting folder on the E: drive and, as before, try to edit the budget file and save your changes.

Question 6	Why are you able to modify the Budget file on this computer, when you were unable to modify it on the other computer?

13. Typical enterprise sharing guidelines call for all access control to be performed using NTFS permissions, not share permissions. On SVR-MBR-C, modify the share and the NTFS permissions for the Accounting folder you created, to conform to the settings shown in the following table.

User/Group	Share Permissions	NTFS Permissions
Student	Allow Full Control	• Allow Modify • Allow Read & Execute • Allow List Folder Contents • Allow Read • Allow Write
Domain Users	Allow Full Control	• Allow Read & Execute • Allow List Folder Contents • Allow Read
Domain Admins	Allow Full Control	• Allow Full Control

14. Take a screen shot of the Security tab on the Accounting Properties sheet, showing the NTFS permissions assigned to the Student user, by pressing Alt+Prt Scr, and then paste the resulting image into the Lab 4 worksheet file in the page provided by pressing Ctrl+V.

End of exercise. Close any open windows before you begin the next exercise.

Exercise 4.4	Creating Shares with Server Manager
Overview	In Windows Server 2012, you can create shares directly within the Server Manager console, once you have installed the file and iSCSI Services role service. In this exercise, you install that role service and create a new share.
Mindset	Windows Server 2012 is all about providing administrators with new ways to perform familiar tasks. Which method for creating shares do you find preferable?
Completion time	15 minutes

1. On SVR-MBR-C, in Server Manager, click Manage > Add Roles and Features. The Add Roles and Features Wizard appears, displaying the *Before you begin* page.

2. Click Next. The *Select installation type* page appears.

3. Click Next. The *Select destination server* page appears.

4. Click Next. The *Select server roles* page appears.

5. Expand the File and Storage Services role and select the File and iSCSI Services check box.

6. Click Next. The *Select features* page appears.

7. Click Next. The *Confirm installation selections* page appears.

8. Click Install. The wizard installs the role.

9. Click Close. The wizard closes.

10. In Server Manager, two additional items appear in the File and Storage Services submenu. Click Shares. The Shares home page appears (see Figure 4-2).

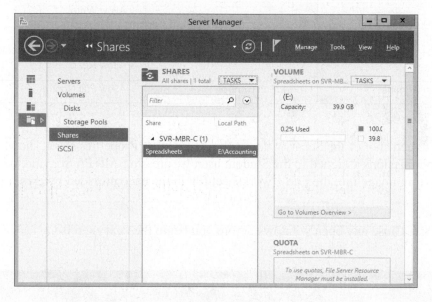

Figure 4-2
The File and Storage Services submenu after the installation of File and iSCSI Services

11. In the Shares tile, click Tasks > New Share. The New Share Wizard appears, displaying the *Select the profile for this share* page.

12. In the *File share profile* list, select SMB Share – Quick and click Next. The *Select the server and path for this share* page appears.

13. In the *Share location* box, select the F: volume and click Next. The *Specify share name* page appears.

14. In the *Share name* text box, type **Documents** and click Next. The *Configure share settings* page appears.

15. Select the *Enable access-based enumeration* check box and click Next. The *Specify permissions to control access* page appears.

16. Click Next to accept the default permissions. The *Confirm selections* page appears.

Question 7	*What access will the Student user have to the Documents share you are creating? How will the users receive that access?*

17. Click Create. The wizard creates the share and the *View results* page appears.

18. Click Close. The Documents share appears in the Shares tile.

19. Take a screen shot of the Shares home page in Server Manager, showing the two shares you created in this lab, by pressing Alt+Prt Scr, and then paste the resulting image into the Lab 4 worksheet file in the page provided by pressing Ctrl+V.

End of exercise. Close any open windows before you begin the next exercise.

Lab Challenge	Creating Shares with Windows PowerShell
Overview	In addition to the graphical tools provided with Windows Server 2012, you can also manipulate the storage subsystem using Windows PowerShell commands.
Completion time	15 minutes

To complete this challenge, specify the Windows PowerShell command you must use to create a new share called *Xfer* out of the Users folder on the C: drive. Configure the share permissions so that members of the Domain Admins group have Full Access and the members of the Domain Users group have Read access.

End of lab.

LAB 5
CONFIGURING PRINT AND DOCUMENT SERVICES

THIS LAB CONTAINS THE FOLLOWING EXERCISES AND ACTIVITIES:

Exercise 5.1   Installing a Printer

Exercise 5.2   Deploying Printers Using Active Directory

Exercise 5.3   Scheduling Printer Access

Lab Challenge   Creating a Printer Pool

BEFORE YOU BEGIN

The lab environment consists of computers connected to a local area network, along with a server that functions as the domain controller for a domain called *adatum.com*. The computers required for this lab are listed in Table 5-1.

Table 5-1
Computers Required for Lab 5

Computer	Operating System	Computer Name
Domain controller	Windows Server 2012	SVR-DC-A
Member server	Windows Server 2012	SVR-MBR-B

In addition to the computers, you also require the software listed in Table 5-2 to complete Lab 5.

Table 5-2
Software Required for Lab 5

Software	Location
Lab 5 student worksheet	Lab05_worksheet.docx (provided by instructor)

Working with Lab Worksheets

Each lab in this manual requires that you answer questions, create screen shots, and perform other activities that you will document in a worksheet named for the lab, such as Lab05_worksheet.docx. It is recommended that you use a USB flash drive to store your worksheets, so you can submit them to your instructor for review. As you perform the exercises in each lab, open the appropriate worksheet file, fill in the required information, and save the file to your flash drive.

After completing this lab, you will be able to:

- Use the Print Management console

- Install a printer

- Deploy printers to workstations

- Control access to printers

Estimated lab time: 75–100 minutes

Exercise 5.1	Installing a Printer
Overview	In this exercise, you install the Print and Document Services role and use the Print Management console included in Windows Server 2012.
Mindset	The Print Management console enables administrators to deploy and manage printers all over the network.
Completion time	10–20 minutes

1. Log on to the SVR-MBR-B computer, using the domain Administrator account and the password **Pa$$w0rd**. In Server Manager, click Manage > Add Roles and Features. The Add Roles and Features Wizard appears, displaying the *Before you begin* page.

2. Click Next. The *Select installation type* page appears.

3. Click Next. The *Select destination server* page appears.

4. Click Next. Select the Print and Document Services check box. The *Add features that are required for Print and Document Services* dialog box appears.

5. Click Add Features. Then click Next. The *Select features* page appears.

6. Click Next. The *Print and Document Services* page appears.

7. Click Next. The *Select role services* page appears.

8. Click Next to accept the default selections. The *Confirm installation selections* page appears.

9. Click Install. The wizard installs the role.

10. Click Close. The wizard closes.

11. In Server Manager, click Tools > Print Management. The Print Management console appears (see Figure 5-1).

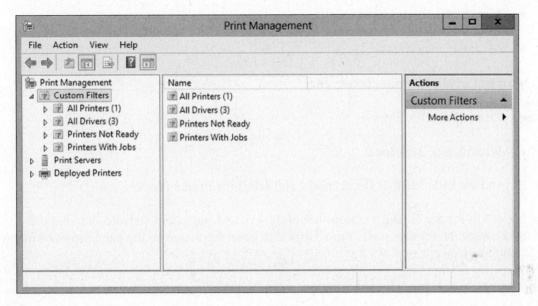

Figure 5-1
Print Management console

12. Expand the Print Servers node, and then right-click the SVR-MBR-B (local) node representing the server. From the context menu, select Add Printer. The Network Printer Installation Wizard appears.

13. Select the Add A New Printer Using An Existing Port option, and leave the LPT1: (Printer Port) value selected. Then click Next. The *Printer Driver* page appears.

14. Leave the Install A New Driver option selected, and click Next. The *Printer Installation* page appears.

15. In the Manufacturer list, select Generic.

16. In the Printers list, select MS Publisher Color Printer, and click Next. The *Printer Name And Sharing Settings* page appears.

17. In the Printer Name text box, type **MSColor**.

18. Leave the Share This Printer check box selected and, in the Share Name text box, type **MSColor**. Then click Next. The *Printer Found* page appears.

Question 1	Why is the wizard able to install the printer when an actual print device is not connected to the computer?

19. Click Next. The *Completing The Network Printer Installation Wizard* page appears.

20. After the printer is installed, click Finish.

21. Repeat the process to install a second printer, using the following settings:

   - Port: LPT2

   - Manufacturer: Generic

   - Printer: MS Publisher Imagesetter

   - Printer Name: MSMono

   - Share Name: MSMono

22. Expand the SVR-MBR-B (local) node, and select the Printers node.

23. Press Alt+Prt Scr to take a screen shot of the Print Management console showing the contents of the Printers node. Press Ctrl+V to paste the image on the page provided in the Lab 5 worksheet file.

End of exercise. You can leave the windows open for the next exercise.

Exercise 5.2	Deploying Printers Using Active Directory
Overview	In this exercise, you use two methods to deploy the printers you created in Windows Server 2012.
Mindset	To simplify network printer deployments, you can publish printer connections to Active Directory Domain Services using Group Policy.
Completion time	10–20 minutes

1. On the SVR-MBR-B computer, in the Print Management console, right-click the MSColor printer and, from the context menu, select List In Directory.

2. Right-click the MSMono printer and, from the context menu, select Deploy With Group Policy. The Deploy with Group Policy dialog box appears (see Figure 5-2).

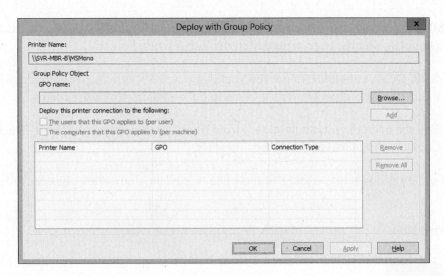

Figure 5-2
The Deploy with Group Policy dialog box

3. Click Browse. The *Browse for a Group Policy Object* dialog box appears.

4. Select Default Domain Policy, and click OK. Default Domain Policy appears in the GPO Name field.

5. Select the check box for The Computers That This GPO Applies To (Per Machine), and click Add. The printer appears in the deployment list.

6. Click OK. A Print Management message box appears, indicating that the printer deployment has succeeded.

7. Click OK twice to close the message box and the Deploy with Group Policy dialog box.

8. Log on to the SVR-DC-A computer, using the domain Administrator account and the password **Pa$$w0rd**. Click the Windows PowerShell button on the taskbar. An *Administrator: Windows PowerShell* window appears.

9. At the Windows PowerShell prompt, type **control /nameMicrosoft.DevicesAndPrinters** and press Enter. The Devices and Printers window appears. (Note: It might be necessary to wait several minutes and click Refresh before the new printer appears.)

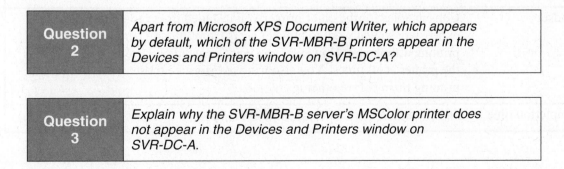

Question 2	Apart from Microsoft XPS Document Writer, which appears by default, which of the SVR-MBR-B printers appear in the Devices and Printers window on SVR-DC-A?

Question 3	Explain why the SVR-MBR-B server's MSColor printer does not appear in the Devices and Printers window on SVR-DC-A.

10. Press Alt+Prt Scr to take a screen shot of the Devices and Printers window. Press Ctrl+V to paste the image on the page provided in the Lab 5 worksheet file.

11. On the SVR-DC-A computer, in Server Manager, click Tools > Active Directory Users and Computers. The Active Directory Users and Computers window appears.

12. Right-click the adatum.com domain and, from the context menu, select Find. The Find Users, Contacts, And Groups dialog box appears.

13. In the Find drop-down list, select Printers. The title of the dialog box changes to Find Printers.

14. Click Find Now.

Question 4	What printers appear in the Search Results box?

15. Right-click the MSColor printer and, from the context menu, select Connect.

16. Switch to the Devices and Printers window.

Question 5	What changed in the Devices and Printers window?

17. Press Alt+Prt Scr to take a screen shot of the Devices and Printers window, showing the latest change. Press Ctrl+V to paste the image on the page provided in the Lab 5 worksheet file.

18. Close the Devices and Printers window and the Find Printers window.

End of exercise. You can leave any windows open for the next exercise.

Exercise 5.3	Scheduling Printer Access
Overview	In this exercise, you configure a printer you installed previously to limit its access to specific individuals and times.
Mindset	Consumables for the color printer you installed in Exercise 5.1 are expensive, so you want to prevent users from running personal jobs or printing after hours. However, you want selected users to be able to access the printer at all times. You also want to prioritize those users' print jobs, printing them before other users' jobs.
Completion time	10–20 minutes

1. On SVR-MBR-B, in the Print Management console, add a second printer for the MS Publisher Color Printer print device you installed in Exercise 5.1. Use the following settings:

    - Port: LPT1

    - Printer Driver: MS Publisher Color Printer

    - Manufacturer: Generic

    - Printer: MS Publisher Color Printer

    - Printer Name: MSColor-PM

    - Share Name: MSColor-PM

2. Select the Printers node in the console, right-click the MSColor printer you created previously, and, in the context menu, select Properties. The MSColor Properties sheet appears.

3. Click the Advanced tab (see Figure 5-3).

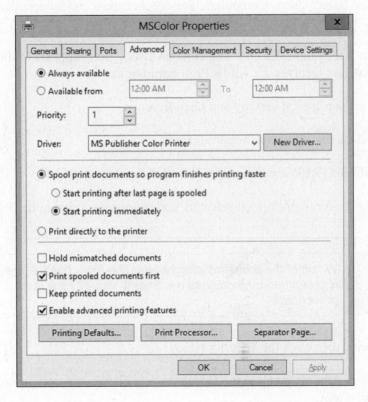

Figure 5-3
The Advanced tab of a printer's Properties sheet

4. Select the Available from option and, in the two spin boxes, select the hours 9:00 AM and 5:00 PM.

Question 6	Which of the problems described in the Exercise 5.3 overview will this setting prevent? How is it prevented?

Question 7	In some instances, a user deliberately or accidently interrupts a print job, stalling the queue until the partial job is removed. Which of the parameters on the Advanced page of a printer's Properties sheet can prevent these interruptions from occurring?

Question 8	When users send print jobs requiring a paper size that is not available, the entire print queue halts until someone inserts the correct paper for that job. Which of the parameters on the Advanced page of a printer's Properties sheet can prevent the queue from being halted?

5. Click Apply, and then click the Security tab.

6. Click Add. The Select Users, Computers, Service Accounts, or Groups dialog box appears.

7. Type **Domain Users** and click OK. The Domain Users group appears in the *Group or user names* list, and receives the Allow Print permission.

8. Select the Everyone special identity and click Remove.

9. Click OK to close the MSColor Properties sheet.

10. Open the MSColor-PM Properties sheet, and click the Advanced tab.

11. Leave the Always Available option selected, and change the value in the Priority spin box to 99.

Question 9	Which of the problems described in the Exercise 5.3 overview is prevented by modifying the Priority value? How is it prevented?

12. Click Apply, and then click the Security tab.

13. Add the Domain Admins group to the Group or User Names list, and grant the Allow Print permission to it.

14. Remove the Everyone special identity from the Group or User Names list.

Question 10	*How do these permission modifications achieve the goals stated in the exercise overview?*

15. Press Alt+Prt Scr to take a screen shot of the Security tab in the MSColor-PM Properties sheet. Press Ctrl+V to paste the image on the page provided in the Lab 5 worksheet file.

16. Click OK to close the MSColor-PM Properties sheet.

End of exercise. Close any open windows before you begin the next exercise.

Lab Challenge	Creating a Printer Pool
Overview	To process a large quantity of print jobs with a single printer, you can create a printer pool, which distributes the print jobs among multiple print devices.
Completion time	20 minutes

To support the Legal department at Contoso, Ltd., your supervisor purchased five identical HP LaserJet 4250 printers to be used as a printer pool. Unlike the printers you installed previously in this lab, which connected to the server using LPT ports, these five printers have Hewlett Packard JetDirect network interface adapters that have already been assigned the following IP addresses:

- 10.0.0.220

- 10.0.0.221

- 10.0.0.222

- 10.0.0.223

- 10.0.0.224

To complete this challenge, add a printer on your server, and share it using the name HPLJ4250 Pool. Then, configure the printer to function as a printer pool using the IP addresses cited previously. Write the procedure you use to create and configure the printer pool, and then take a screen shot of the Ports tab in the HPLJ4250 Pool Properties sheet. Paste the image in the Lab 5 worksheet file.

End of lab.

LAB 6
CONFIGURING SERVERS FOR REMOTE MANAGEMENT

THIS LAB CONTAINS THE FOLLOWING EXERCISES AND ACTIVITIES:

Exercise 6.1   Adding Servers to Server Manager

Exercise 6.2   Working with Remote Servers

Lab Challenge   Configuring Windows Firewall

Exercise 6.3   Using Remote Server Administration Tools

BEFORE YOU BEGIN

The lab environment consists of computers connected to a local area network, along with a server that functions as the domain controller for a domain called *adatum.com*. The computers required for this lab are listed in Table 6-1.

Table 6-1
Computers Required for Lab 6

Computer	Operating System	Computer Name
Domain controller	Windows Server 2012	SVR-DC-A
Member server	Windows Server 2012	SVR-MBR-B
Member server	Windows Server 2012	SVR-MBR-C

In addition to the computers, you also require the software listed in Table 6-2 to complete Lab 6.

Table 6-2
Software Required for Lab 6

Software	Location
Lab 6 student worksheet	Lab06_worksheet.docx (provided by instructor)

Working with Lab Worksheets

Each lab in this manual requires that you answer questions, take screen shots, and perform other activities that you will document in a worksheet named for the lab, such as Lab06_worksheet.docx. It is recommended that you use a USB flash drive to store your worksheets, so you can submit them to your instructor for review. As you perform the exercises in each lab, open the appropriate worksheet file, fill in the required information, and save the file to your flash drive.

After completing this lab, you will be able to:

- Configure Server Manager to administer multiple servers

- Use the Remote Server Administration Tools to manage a domain controller

- Install roles and features on a remote server

Estimated lab time: 75 minutes

Exercise 6.1	Adding Servers to Server Manager
Overview	In this exercise, you add servers to a member server's Server Manager interface, so you can install roles and features on any server, as well as perform other administration tasks.
Mindset	How do you use the Server Manager application on a single computer to manage multiple servers?
Completion time	10 minutes

1. On the SVR-MBR-C computer, log on using the domain **Administrator** account, with the password **Pa$$w0rd**. The Server Manager console appears.

2. In the left pane, click All Servers. The All Servers home page appears, displaying only the local server.

3. Right-click the All Servers icon and, from the context menu, select Add Servers. The Add Servers dialog box appears.

4. With the Active Directory tab and the adatum domain selected, click Find Now. The three servers on the network appear (see Figure 6-1).

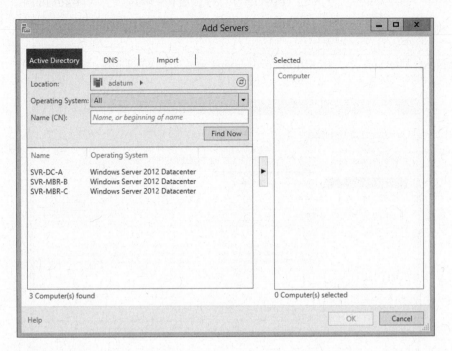

Figure 6-1
The Add Servers dialog box in Server Manager

5. Select the SVR-DC-A server and click the right arrow. The server appears in the Selected list.

6. Select the SVR-MBR-B server and click the right arrow. The server appears in the Selected list.

7. Click OK. The wizard closes and the two remote servers appear in the Servers tile.

8. Press Alt+Prt Scr to take a screen shot of the Server Manager console showing the Servers tile with the servers you just added. Press Ctrl+V to paste the image on the page provided in the Lab 6 worksheet file.

End of exercise. You can leave the windows open for the next exercise.

Exercise 6.2	Working with Remote Servers
Overview	In this exercise, you use Server Manager to connect to another server on the network and try to access the Computer Management console.
Mindset	How do you use the Server Manager application on a single computer to manage multiple servers?
Completion time	20 minutes

1. Log on to the SVR-MBR-C computer, using the domain Administrator account and the password **Pa$$w0rd**. In Server Manager, click Manage > Add Roles and Features. The Add Roles and Features Wizard appears, displaying the *Before you begin* page.

2. Click Next. The *Select installation type* page appears.

3. Click Next. The *Select destination server* page appears (see Figure 6-2).

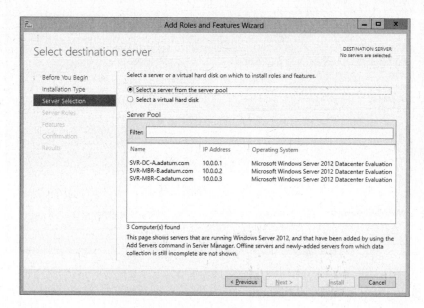

Figure 6-2
The *Select destination server* page in Server Manager

4. Select the SVR-MBR-B.adatum.com server in the Server Pool list and click Next. The *Select server roles* page appears.

5. Select the Web Server (IIS) check box. The *Add features that are required for Web Server (IIS)* dialog box appears.

6. Click Add Features. Then click Next. The *Select features* page appears.

7. Click Next. The *Web Server Role (IIS)* page appears.

8. Click Next. The *Select role services* page appears.

9. Click Next to accept the default role services. The *Confirm installation selections* page appears.

10. Select the *Restart the destination server automatically if required* check box and click Install. The *Installation progress* page appears as the wizard installs the role on the remote system.

11. Click Close. The wizard closes.

12. In Server Manager, click the Tools menu.

Question 1	Why does the Internet Information Services (IIS) Manager console not appear in the Tools menu if you have previously installed the Web Server (IIS) role?

13. On SVR-MBR-B, log on using the domain **Administrator** account and the password **Pa$$w0rd**.

Question 2	How can you tell that the Web Server (IIS) role has been successfully installed on the remote server?

14. Press Alt+Prt Scr to take a screen shot of the Server Manager console on SVR-MBR-B, showing the Web Server (IIS) role has been installed. Press Ctrl+V to paste the image on the page provided in the Lab 6 worksheet file.

15. On SVR-MBR-C, in Server Manager, click the All Servers icon. The All Servers home page appears.

16. In the Servers tile, right-click the SVR-MBR-B server and, from the context menu, select Restart Server. A message box appears, prompting you to confirm that you want to restart the server.

17. Click OK. Server SVR-MBR-B restarts.

18. In the Servers tile, right-click the SVR-MBR-B server and, from the context menu, select Computer Management. An Event Viewer message box appears, informing you that the Computer Management console cannot connect to SVR-MBR-B. Click OK.

Question 3	What must you do to enable the Computer Management console to connect to SVR-MBR-B?

End of exercise. Close any open windows before you begin the next exercise.

Lab Challenge	Configuring Windows Firewall
Overview	Although Server Manager can install roles and perform certain management functions on remote servers, the default Windows Firewall settings prevent Microsoft Management Console (MMC) snap-ins from connecting to remote servers.
Completion time	15 minutes

To complete this lab, you must configure Windows Firewall on SVR-MBR-B so that the Computer Management console running on SVR-MBR-C can connect to SVR-MBR-B. Then, on SVR-MBR-C, press Alt+Prt Scr to take a screen shot of the Computer Management console on SVR-MBR-B, after selecting Event Viewer in the left pane, showing the connection to the remote server. Press Ctrl+V to paste the image on the page provided in the Lab 6 worksheet file.

End of exercise. Close any open windows before you begin the next exercise.

Exercise 6.3	Using Remote Server Administration Tools
Overview	In this exercise, you install the Remote Server Administration Tools feature and use it to manage the other servers on your network.
Mindset	Where are your domain controllers? According to Microsoft's recommendations, they should be under lock and key, and administrators should access them remotely.
Completion time	15 minutes

1. On the SVR-MBR-C computer, in Server Manager, click Tools. Select one of the Active Directory Domain Services administration tools. The Tools menu appears (see Figure 6-3).

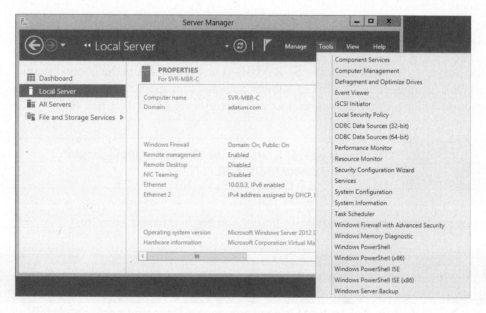

Figure 6-3
The Tools menu on a member server

Question 4	Why do the standard Active Directory Domain Services administration tools not appear in the Tools menu?

2. In Server Manager, click Manage > Add Roles and Features. The Add Roles and Features Wizard appears, displaying the *Before you begin* page.

3. Click Next. The *Select installation type* page appears.

4. Click Next. The *Select destination server* page appears.

5. Select SVR-MBR-C, and then click Next. The *Select server roles* page appears.

6. Click Next. The *Select features* page appears.

7. Scroll down and expand the Remote Server Administration Tools feature.

8. Expand the Role Administration Tools feature and select the AD DS and AD LDS Tools check box.

9. Click Next. The *Confirm installation selections* page appears.

10. Click Install. The *Installation progress* page appears as the wizard installs the selected features.

11. Click Close. The wizard closes.

12. Click Tools. The Tools menu appears, which now contains the Active Directory administration tools.

13. Press Alt+Prt Scr to take a screen shot of the Tools menu. Press Ctrl+V to paste the image on the page provided in the Lab 6 worksheet file.

End of lab.

LAB 7
CREATING AND CONFIGURING VIRTUAL MACHINE SETTINGS

THIS LAB CONTAINS THE FOLLOWING EXERCISES AND ACTIVITIES:

Exercise 7.1   Installing the Hyper-V Role

Exercise 7.2   Creating a Virtual Machine

Lab Challenge   Creating a Virtual Machine Using Windows PowerShell

Exercise 7.3   Configuring Dynamic Memory

Lab Challenge   Configuring Dynamic Memory Using Windows PowerShell

BEFORE YOU BEGIN

The lab environment consists of three servers connected to a local area network, which is configured to function as the domain controller for a domain called *adatum.com*. The computers required for this lab are listed in Table 7-1.

Table 7-1
Computers Required for Lab 7

Computer	Operating System	Computer Name
Domain controller 1	Windows Server 2012	SVR-DC-A
Member server 2	Windows Server 2012	SVR-MBR-B
Member server 3	Windows Server 2012	SVR-MBR-C

In addition to the computers, you also require the software listed in Table 7-2 to complete Lab 7.

Table 7-2
Software Required for Lab 7

Software	Location
Lab 7 student worksheet	Lab07_worksheet.docx (provided by instructor)

Working with Lab Worksheets

Each lab in this manual requires that you answer questions, take screen shots, and perform other activities that you will document in a worksheet named for the lab, such as Lab07_worksheet.docx. It is recommended that you use a USB flash drive to store your worksheets, so you can submit them to your instructor for review. As you perform the exercises in each lab, open the appropriate worksheet file, fill in the required information, and save the file to your flash drive.

After completing this lab, you will be able to:

- Install Hyper-V

- Create Hyper-V virtual machines

- Configure VMs to use dynamic memory

Estimated lab time: 50 minutes

Exercise 7.1	Installing the Hyper-V Role
Overview	In this exercise, you use the Add Roles and Features Wizard to install the Hyper-V role on one of your member servers.
Mindset	What hardware is necessary to run Hyper-V?
Completion time	10 minutes

1. Log on to the SVR-MBR-B computer, using the domain Administrator account and the password **Pa$$w0rd**. Click the Windows PowerShell button on the taskbar. An Administrator: Windows PowerShell window appears.

2. At the Windows PowerShell prompt, type the following command and press Enter:

   DISM /online /enable-feature /featurename:Microsoft-Hyper-V

3. The system installs the Hyper-V role and prompts you to restart the server (see Figure 7-1).

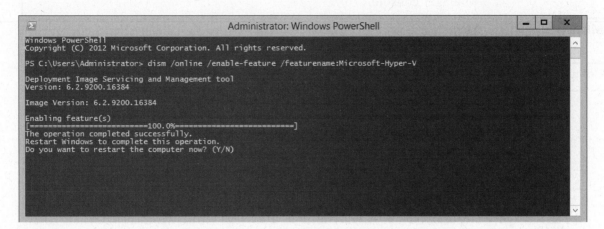

Figure 7-1
Prompt to restart the server

4. Press Y. The system restarts.

5. Log on to SVR-MBR-B using the domain **Administrator** account and the password **Pa$$w0rd**. The Server Manager console opens.

6. In the Server Manager console, select Manage > Add Roles and Features. The Add Roles and Features Wizard appears, displaying the *Before you begin* page.

7. Click Next. The *Select Installation Type* page appears.

8. Leave the *Role-based or feature-based installation* radio button selected and click Next. The *Select Destination Server* page appears.

9. Click Next to accept the default local server. The *Select Server Roles* page appears.

10. Click Next. The *Select features* page appears.

11. Expand Remote Server Administration Tools and Role Administration Tools and select the Hyper-V Management Tools check box.

12. Click Next. The Confirm installation selections page appears.

13. Click Install. The *Installation Progress* page appears as the wizard installs the Hyper-V role.

14. Click Close. The Add Roles and Features Wizard closes.

End of exercise. You can leave the windows open for the next exercise.

Exercise 7.2	Creating a Virtual Machine
Overview	In this exercise, you create a new virtual machine using the Hyper-V Manager console.
Mindset	How does Hyper-V provide resources that are virtual equivalents of physical hardware?
Completion time	10 minutes

1. On the SVR-MBR-B computer, which has the Server Manager console open, select Tools >Hyper-V Manager. The Hyper-V Manager console appears.

2. In the left pane, select the SVR-MBR-B node.

3. In the right pane, click New > Virtual Machine. The New Virtual Machine Wizard appears, displaying the *Before You Begin* page.

4. Click Next. The *Specify Name and Location* page appears.

5. In the Name text box, type **Vmachine1** and click Next. The *Assign Memory* page appears.

6. In the Startup memory text box, type **128** and click Next. The *Configure Networking* page appears.

> **NOTE**
>
> *The memory amounts used in this exercise are intended for demonstration purposes only. They are insufficient to run virtual machines with Windows guest operating systems.*

> **Question 1**
>
> *Why are you unable to connect this virtual machine to a network?*

7. Click Next. The *Connect Virtual Hard Disk* page appears.

8. Click Next. The *Installation Options* page appears.

9. Click Next. The *Completing the New Virtual Machine Wizard* page appears.

10. Click Finish. The wizard creates the new virtual machine, and it appears in the Hyper-V Manager console.

End of exercise. You can leave the windows open for the next exercise.

Question 2	*Why would a virtual machine in this default configuration fail to boot if you were to start it?*

Lab Challenge	Creating a VM with Windows PowerShell
Overview	To complete this challenge, you must create a virtual machine using Windows PowerShell commands, as you would on a Server Core installation.
Completion time	10 minutes

Create a new Hyper-V virtual machine named **Vmachine2**, with a 127 GB virtual hard disk and 512 MB of startup memory using the same default settings as the one you created with the New Virtual Machine Wizard in Exercise 7.2.

Write out the Windows PowerShell command(s) that will execute the required settings. Then, take a screen shot of the Hyper-V Manager console showing the two VMs you created, Vmachine1 and Vmachine2, by pressing Alt+Prt Scr, and then paste the resulting image into the Lab 7 worksheet file in the page provided by pressing Ctrl+V.

End of exercise. You can leave the windows open for the next exercise.

Exercise 7.3	Configuring Dynamic Memory
Overview	In this exercise, you configure your virtual machine to use Dynamic Memory, enabling it to assign itself additional memory as needed.
Mindset	How can you tell how much memory a virtual machine needs at any given time?
Completion time	10 minutes

1. On the SVR-MBR-B computer, in the Hyper-V Manager console, select the Vmachine1 virtual machine you created previously and, in the right pane, click Settings. The *Settings for Vmachine1 on SVR-MBR-B* dialog box appears.

2. In the Hardware list, click the Memory icon. The Memory page appears (see Figure 7-2).

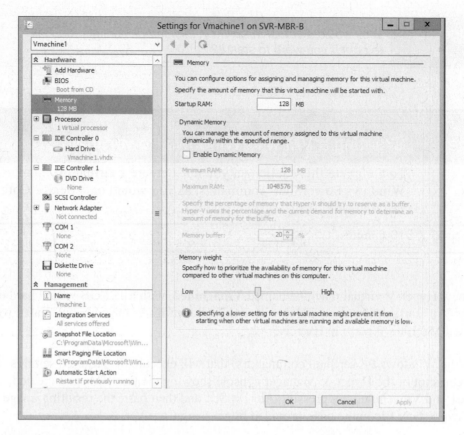

Figure 7-2
The Memory page of the Settings dialog box

3. In the *Startup RAM* text box, type **256**.

Question 3	What is the maximum amount of memory that Vmachine1 can use in its current configuration with Startup RAM set to 1024 megabytes?

4. Select the *Enable Dynamic Memory* check box to enable the Dynamic Memory controls.

5. In the Minimum RAM text box, type **128** and in the Maximum RAM text box, type **480**.

Question 4	Why is it possible for the Minimum RAM value to be smaller than the Startup RAM value?

6. In the Memory Buffer spin box, set the value to **50**%.

Question 5	Will increasing the Memory Buffer value on all of your virtual machines enable the Hyper-V server to run more or fewer VMs? Why?

7.   Increase the Memory Weight value by pushing the slider all the way to the right.

Question 6	How will increasing the Memory Weight value on all of a Hyper-V server's virtual machines to the maximum affect their performance?

8.   Click OK to close the Settings for Vmachine1 on SVR-MBR-B dialog box.

End of exercise. You can leave the windows open for the next exercise.

Lab Challenge	Configuring Dynamic Memory Using Windows PowerShell
Overview	To complete this challenge, you must configure a virtual machine to use dynamic memory.
Completion time	10 minutes

Using Windows PowerShell commands only, configure the Vmachine2 virtual machine you created in the previous challenge to use dynamic memory, using the same values you assigned to Vmachine1 in Exercise 7.3.

Write out the Windows PowerShell command(s) that will apply the required settings. Then, after you execute the commands, use Windows PowerShell to display the dynamic memory settings and take a screen shot of the display by pressing Alt+Prt Scr. Paste the resulting image into the Lab 7 worksheet file in the page provided by pressing Ctrl+V.

End of lab

LAB 8
CREATING AND CONFIGURING VIRTUAL MACHINE STORAGE

THIS LAB CONTAINS THE FOLLOWING EXERCISES AND ACTIVITIES: _ _ _ _

Exercise 8.1   Creating a Virtual Hard Disk

Exercise 8.2   Editing a Virtual Hard Disk File

Exercise 8.3   Creating a Virtual Machine with an Existing Virtual Hard Disk

Exercise 8.4   Creating a Pass-Through Disk

Lab Challenge   Creating a Snapshot

BEFORE YOU BEGIN

The lab environment consists of three servers connected to a local area network, one of which is configured to function as the domain controller for a domain called *adatum.com*. The computers required for this lab are listed in Table 8-1.

Table 8-1
Computers Required for Lab 8

Computer	Operating System	Computer Name
Domain controller 1	Windows Server 2012	SVR-DC-A
Member server 2	Windows Server 2012	SVR-MBR-B
Member server 3	Windows Server 2012	SVR-MBR-C

In addition to the computers, you also require the software listed in Table 8-2 to complete Lab 8.

Table 8-2
Software Required for Lab 8

Software	Location
Lab 8 student worksheet	Lab08_worksheet.docx (provided by instructor)

Working with Lab Worksheets

Each lab in this manual requires that you answer questions, take screen shots, and perform other activities that you will document in a worksheet named for the lab, such as Lab08_worksheet.docx. It is recommended that you use a USB flash drive to store your worksheets, so you can submit them to your instructor for review. As you perform the exercises in each lab, open the appropriate worksheet file, fill in the required information, and save the file to your flash drive.

After completing this lab, you will be able to:

- Create and edit VHDxs

- Create VM with existing VHDx

- Create a pass-through drive

Estimated lab time: 50 minutes

Exercise 8.1	Creating a Virtual Hard Disk
Overview	In this exercise, you use the Hyper-V Management console to create a new virtual hard disk.
	What hardware options are available when creating virtual hard disks in Hyper-V?
Completion time	10 minutes

1. Log on to the SVR-MBR-B computer, which has the Hyper-V role installed, using the domain Administrator account and the password **Pa$$w0rd**. In the Server Manager console, select Tools > Hyper-V Manager. The Hyper-V Manager console appears.

2. In the left pane, click SVR-MBR-B, and then in the right pane, click New > Hard Disk. The New Virtual Hard Disk Wizard appears, displaying the *Before You Begin* page.

3. Click Next. The *Choose Disk Format* page appears.

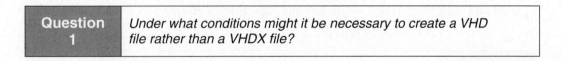

Question 1	Under what conditions might it be necessary to create a VHD file rather than a VHDX file?

4. Click Next to accept the default VHDX value. The *Choose Disk Type* page appears (see Figure 8-1).

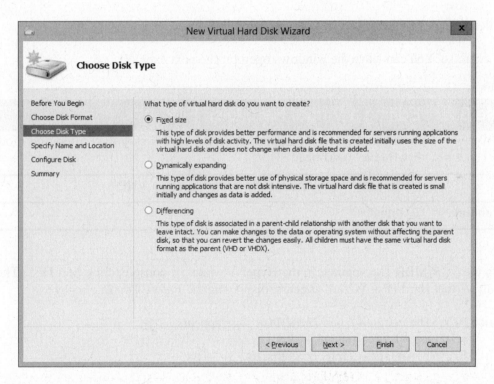

Figure 8-1
The *Choose Disk Type* page

5. Select the Fixed size option and click Next. The *Specify Name and Location* page appears.

Question 2	*If you choose to create a differencing drive rather than a fixed size drive, you must specify a name for the new disk and also identify a parent disk. What happens to the parent disk as a result of creating the differencing disk?*

6. In the Name text box, type **Fixed1** and click Next. The *Configure Disk* page appears.

7. Leave the *Create a new blank virtual hard disk* option selected and, in the Size text box, type **20** and click Next. The *Completing the New Virtual Hard Disk Wizard* page appears.

Question 3	*If you were to select the* Copy the contents of the specified physical *disk option and then select one of the listed physical disks, would you or would you not be creating a pass-through disk?*

8. Click Finish. The wizard creates the new virtual disk file.

End of exercise. You can leave the windows open for the next exercise.

Exercise 8.2	Editing a Virtual Hard Disk File
Overview	In this exercise, you open the virtual hard disk you created and modify it while it's offline.
Mindset	Under what conditions is it necessary to edit a VHD?
Completion time	10 minutes

1. On the SVR-MBR-B computer, in the Hyper-V Manager console, click Edit Disk. The Edit Virtual Hard Disk Wizard appears, displaying the *Before You Begin* page.

2. Click Next. The *Locate Virtual Hard Disk* page appears.

3. Click Browse. An Open combo box appears.

4. Select the Fixed1.vhdx virtual hard disk you created in Exercise 8.1 and click Open (see Figure 8-2).

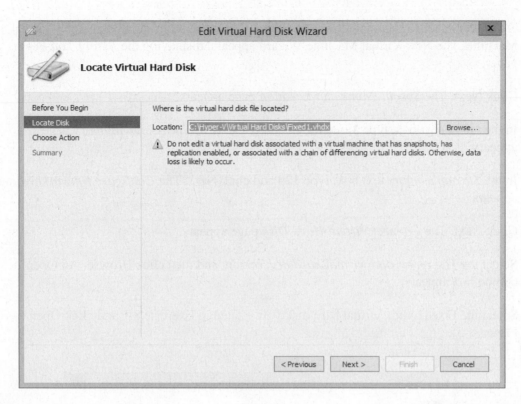

Figure 8-2
The *Locate Virtual Hard Disk* page

5. Click Next. The *Choose Action* page appears.

6. Select the Expand option and click Next. The *Expand Virtual Hard Disk* page appears.

7. In the New Size text box, type **25** and click Next. The *Completing the Edit Virtual Hard Disk Wizard* page appears.

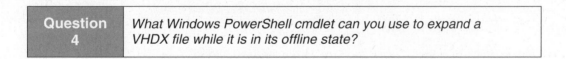

Question 4	*What Windows PowerShell cmdlet can you use to expand a VHDX file while it is in its offline state?*

8. Click Finish. The wizard expands the file and closes it.

End of exercise. You can leave the windows open for the next exercise.

Exercise 8.3	Creating a VM with an Existing Virtual Hard Disk
Overview	In this exercise, you create a new virtual machine using an existing VHD.
Mindset	How do you mount an existing VHD into a new virtual machine?
Completion time	10 minutes

1. On the SVR-MBR-B computer, in the Hyper-V Manager console, click New > Virtual Machine. The New Virtual Machine Wizard appears, displaying the *Before You Begin* page.

2. Click Next. The *Specify Name and Location* page appears.

3. In the Name text box, type **Vmachine3** and click Next. The *Assign Memory* page appears.

4. In the *Startup memory* text box, type **128** and click Next. The *Configure Networking* page appears.

5. Click Next. The *Connect Virtual Hard Disk* page appears.

6. Select the *Use an existing virtual hard disk* option, and then click Browse. An Open combo box appears.

7. Select the Fixed1.vhdx virtual hard disk you created in Exercise 8.1 and click Open (see Figure 8-3).

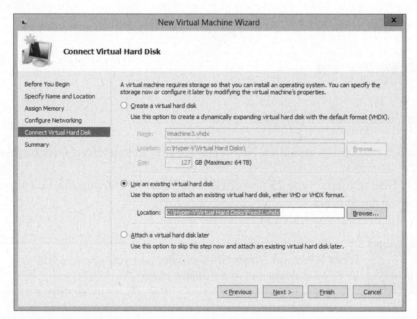

Figure 8-3
The *Connect Virtual Hard Disk* page

8. Click Next. The Completing the New Virtual Machine Wizard page appears.

Question 5	Why doesn't the Installation Options page appear at this time, as it did when you ran the New Virtual Machine Wizard in Lab 7?

9. Click Finish. The wizard creates the new virtual machine, and it appears in the Hyper-V Manager console.

End of exercise. You can leave the windows open for the next exercise.

Exercise 8.4	Creating a Pass-Through Disk
Overview	In this exercise, you configure a virtual machine to use a physical disk in the host computer, rather than a VHD.
Mindset	Under what conditions would you want to use a pass-through disk, rather than a virtual hard disk?
Completion time	15 minutes

1. Log on to the SVR-MBR-C computer, using the domain Administrator account and the password **Pa$$w0rd**. In Server Manager, click Tools > Hyper-V Manager. The Hyper-V Manager console appears.

2. In the right pane, click New > Virtual Machine. The New Virtual Machine Wizard appears, displaying the *Before You Begin* page.

3. Click Next. The *Specify Name and Location* page appears.

4. In the Name text box, type **Vmachine4** and click Next. The *Assign Memory* page appears.

5. In the *Startup memory* text box, type **128** and click Next. The *Configure Networking* page appears.

6. Click Next. The *Connect Virtual Hard Disk* page appears.

7. Select the *Attach a virtual hard disk later* option and click Next. The *Installation Options* page appears.

8. Click Next. The *Completing the New Virtual Machine Wizard* page appears.

9. Click Finish. The wizard creates the new virtual machine, and it appears in the Hyper-V Manager console.

10. Select the Vmachine4 virtual machine you just created and, in the right pane, click Settings. The *Settings for Vmachine4 on SVR-MBR-C* dialog box appears.

11. In the Hardware list, click the *IDE Controller 0* node. On the right side of the dialog box, select Hard Drive and click Add. The *Hard Drive* page appears.

12. Select the *Physical hard disk* option to create a pass-through disk. However, the drop-down list does not contain any drives, so you cannot create a pass-through disk.

13. Click Cancel to close the Settings dialog box.

14. In Server Manager, click Tools > Computer Management. The Computer Management console appears.

15. In the left pane, select the Disk Management node. The Disk Management snap-in appears (see Figure 8-4).

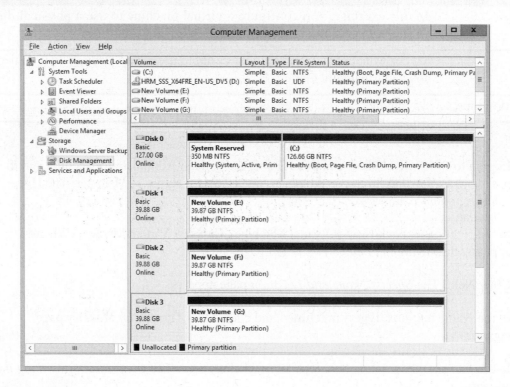

Figure 8-4
The Disk Management snap-in

Question 6	Why don't any of the physical disks in the Disk Management snap-in appear in the Settings dialog box when you attempt to create a pass-through disk?

16. In the Disk Management snap-in, right-click the Disk 3 panel and, from the context menu, select Offline. The status of the disk changes to offline.

17. Close the Computer Management console.

18. Back in the Hyper-V Manager console, open the Settings dialog box for the Vmachine4 VM once again.

19. In the Hardware list, click the *IDE Controller 0* node. On the right-side of the dialog box, select Hard Drive and click Add. The *Hard Drive* page appears.

20. Select the *Physical hard disk* option to create a pass-through disk. This time, the disk you took offline appears in the drop-down list.

21. Select Disk 3 in the drop-down list.

22. Take a screen shot of the Settings dialog box in the Hyper-V Manager console, showing the pass-through disk option, by pressing Alt+Prt Scr, and then paste the resulting image into the Lab 8 worksheet file in the page provided by pressing Ctrl+V.

23. Click OK to close the Settings dialog box.

End of exercise. You can leave the windows open for the next exercise.

Lab Challenge	Creating a Snapshot
Overview	To complete this challenge, you must create a snapshot of a virtual machine, preserving its state at a particular date and time.
Completion time	10 minutes

To complete this challenge, create a snapshot of Vmachine3 on SVR-MBR-B and take a screen shot of the Hyper-V Manager console, showing the snapshot you created, by pressing Alt+Prt Scr, and then paste the resulting image into the Lab 8 worksheet file in the page provided by pressing Ctrl+V.

End of lab.

LAB 9
CREATING AND CONFIGURING VIRTUAL NETWORKS

THIS LAB CONTAINS THE FOLLOWING EXERCISES AND ACTIVITIES: _ _ _ _

Exercise 9.1   Creating a Virtual Switch

Exercise 9.2   Creating a Virtual Network

Lab Challenge   Creating an Isolated Network

BEFORE YOU BEGIN

The lab environment consists of three servers connected to a local area network, one of which is configured to function as the domain controller for a domain called *adatum.com*. The computers required for this lab are listed in Table 9-1.

Table 9-1
Computers Required for Lab 9

Computer	Operating System	Computer Name
Domain controller 1	Windows Server 2012	SVR-DC-A
Member server 2	Windows Server 2012	SVR-MBR-B
Member server 3	Windows Server 2012	SVR-MBR-C

In addition to the computers, you also require the software listed in Table 9-2 to complete Lab 9.

Table 9-2
Software required for Lab 9

Software	Location
Lab 9 student worksheet	Lab09_worksheet.docx (provided by instructor)

Working with Lab Worksheets

Each lab in this manual requires that you answer questions, take screen shots, and perform other activities that you will document in a worksheet named for the lab, such as Lab09_worksheet.docx. It is recommended that you use a USB flash drive to store your worksheets, so you can submit them to your instructor for review. As you perform the exercises in each lab, open the appropriate worksheet file, fill in the required information, and save the file to your flash drive.

After completing this lab, you will be able to:

- Create a virtual switch

- Create a virtual network

- Create an isolated network

Estimated lab time: 45 minutes

Exercise 9.1	Creating a Virtual Switch
Overview	In this exercise, you use the Virtual Switch Manager to create a Hyper-V component that provides the same services to virtual machines as a physical switch does to physical computers.
Mindset	Which type of switch should you create?
Completion time	15 minutes

1. Log on to the SVR-MBR-C computer, which has the Hyper-V role installed, using the domain Administrator account and the password **Pa$$w0rd**. Open the Server Manager console and select Tools > Hyper-V Manager. The Hyper-V Manager console appears.

2. In the left pane, select SVR-MBR-C, and in the right pane, click Virtual Switch Manager. The Virtual Switch Manager for SVR-MBR-C dialog box appears (see Figure 9-1).

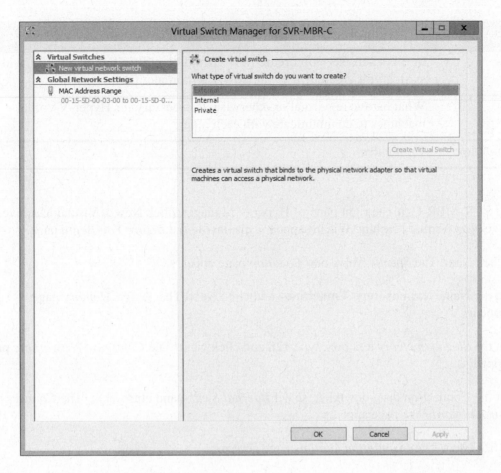

Figure 9-1
The Virtual Switch Manager dialog box

3. In the left pane, select New virtual network switch.

4. In the Create virtual switch page, select Internal and click Create Virtual Switch. The new switch appears in the left pane, selected so that the Virtual Switch Properties page appears in the right pane.

5. In the Name text box, type **Internal Switch** and click OK. The Virtual Switch Manager dialog box closes.

6. Open the Virtual Switch Manager dialog box again and take a screen shot of the dialog box, showing the virtual switch you created, by pressing Alt+Prt Scr, and then paste the resulting image into the Lab 9 worksheet file in the page provided by pressing Ctrl+V.

7. Click OK.

End of exercise. You can leave the windows open for the next exercise.

Exercise 9.2	Creating a Virtual Network
Overview	In this exercise, you create new virtual machines and use the virtual switch you created in Exercise 9.1 to connect them together.
Mindset	What hardware, virtual or otherwise, is necessary for Hyper-V virtual machines to communicate with each other?
Completion time	15 minutes

1. In SVR-MBR-C, in the right pane of Hyper-V Manager, click New > Virtual Machine. The New Virtual Machine Wizard appears, displaying the *Before You Begin* page.

2. Click Next. The *Specify Name and Location* page appears.

3. In the Name text box, type **Vmachine4** and click Next. The *Assign Memory* page appears.

4. In the *Startup memory* text box, type **128** and click Next. The *Configure Networking* page appears.

5. In the Connection drop-down list, select *Internal Switch* and click Next. The *Connect Virtual Hard Disk* page appears.

6. Click Next. The *Installation Options* page appears.

7. Click Next. The *Completing the New Virtual Machine Wizard* page appears.

8. Click Finish. The wizard creates the new virtual machine, and it appears in the Hyper-V Manager console.

9. Repeat steps 1 to 8 to create a second virtual machine, this one named **Vmachine5**.

Question 1	Assuming that the virtual machines you just created have Windows Server 2012 installed on them, in its default configuration, and all of the computers are configured with appropriate IP addresses, what communications would be possible on this virtual network?

Question 2	How would the communication capabilities of the virtual network differ if you had created an external virtual switch instead of an internal one? Why is this so?

10. Take a screen shot of the Hyper-V Manager console, showing the two VMs you created, by pressing Alt+Prt Scr, and then paste the resulting image into the Lab 9 worksheet file in the page provided by pressing Ctrl+V.

End of exercise. You can leave the windows open for the next exercise.

Lab Challenge	Creating an Isolated Network
Overview	To complete this challenge, you must use Windows PowerShell cmdlets to create and configure the components required to build a virtual network that is completely isolated from all external physical networks and the Hyper-V Host computer.
Completion time	15 minutes

Using Windows PowerShell cmdlets only, you must create a new virtual network connecting the Vmachine4 and Vmachine5 virtual machines you created previously in this lab. The new virtual network must be completely isolated, both from the Hyper-V server hosting the virtual machines and from the physical network to which the server is connected.

To create the new network, you need to create a new virtual switch and add a new network adapter to each of the virtual machines. Write out the Windows PowerShell commands needed to create and configure the required components. Then take a screen shot of the Windows PowerShell interface, showing the commands executed, by pressing Alt+Prt Scr, and then paste the resulting image into the Lab 9 worksheet file in the page provided by pressing Ctrl+V.

Question 3	When connecting a virtual machine to an isolated network, should you install a synthetic network adapter or a legacy network adapter? Explain why.

End of lab.

LAB 10
CONFIGURING IPv4 AND IPv6 ADDRESSING

THIS LAB CONTAINS THE FOLLOWING EXERCISES AND ACTIVITIES: _ _ _ _

Exercise 10.1	Calculating IP Addresses
Exercise 10.2	Manually Configuring TCP/IP
Lab Challenge	Configuring TCP/IP Using Windows PowerShell
Exercise 10.3	Testing Network Connections

BEFORE YOU BEGIN

The lab environment consists of computers connected to a local area network, along with a server that functions as the domain controller for a domain called *adatum.com*. The computers required for this lab are listed in Table 10-1.

Table 10-1
Computers Required for Lab 10

Computer	Operating System	Computer Name
Domain controller	Windows Server 2012	SVR-DC-A
Member server	Windows Server 2012	SVR-MBR-B
Member server	Windows Server 2012	SVR-MBR-C

In addition to the computers, you also require the software listed in Table 10-2 to complete Lab 10.

Table 10-2
Software Required for Lab 10

Software	Location
Lab 10 student worksheet	Lab10_worksheet.docx (provided by instructor)

Working with Lab Worksheets

Each lab in this manual requires that you answer questions, take screen shots, and perform other activities that you will document in a worksheet named for the lab, such as Lab10_worksheet.docx. It is recommended that you use a USB flash drive to store your worksheets, so you can submit them to your instructor for review. As you perform the exercises in each lab, open the appropriate worksheet file, fill in the required information, and save the file to your flash drive.

After completing this lab, you will be able to:

- Calculate network addresses and IP addresses

- Manually configure the Windows Server 2012 TCP/IP client

- Configure TCP/IP using Windows PowerShell

- Test network connections using Ping

Estimated lab time: 60 minutes

Exercise 10.1	Calculating IP Addresses
Overview	In this exercise, you are responsible for subnetting a network to suit a particular network organization plan.
Mindset	What IPv4 addressing policies does your organization have in place?
Completion time	20 minutes

To complete this exercise, you must determine what IPv4 addresses you should use on the workgroup for which you are responsible. Your supervisor has assigned you a group of computers that consists of three servers and seven workstations. Your entire department must share an IPv4 network with the address 192.168.75.0/24, and your supervisor has asked you to subnet that address into as many networks as possible with at least 10 hosts each.

Create a list of the network addresses your subnetting can create, using CIDR notation. Then choose one of the subnets for use by your computers and list the IP addresses in that subnet, along with the correct subnet mask value.

Table 10-3
IPv4 Network Addresses, IP Addresses, and Subnet Mask

IPv4 Network Addresses
IP Addresses
Subnet Mask

The MAC addresses of three computers on your network are listed in Table 10-4. Using these MAC addresses to form interface IDs, create three unique local unicast addresses on the fd00::/8 network and enter them into the table.

Table 10-4
MAC Addresses and IPv6 Addresses

Computer	MAC Address	IPv6 Address
SVR-DC-A	12-AA-BC-32-23-12	
SVR-MBR-B	12-AA-BC-32-23-11	
SVR-MBR-C	00-15-5D-01-01-C1	

End of exercise. You can leave any windows open for the next exercise.

Exercise 10.2	Manually Configuring TCP/IP
Overview	In this exercise, you configure the IP addresses and other TCP/IP configuration parameters for your computers, using the graphical tools in Windows Server 2012.
Mindset	What parameters do you have to configure to ensure that the computers on your network can communicate with each other?
Completion time	20 minutes

1. Using the IP addresses you calculated in Exercise 10.1, specify the values you will use when configuring your computers by filling in the empty cells in the Table 10-5 in your worksheet.

Table 10-5
TCP/IP Configuration Settings for Exercise 10.2

	SVR-DC-A	SVR-MBR-B	SVR-MBR-C
IP Address	192.168.75.81	192.168.75.82	192.168.75.83
Subnet Mask	255.255.255.240	255.255.255.240	255.255.255.240
Preferred DNS Server	192.168.75.81	192.168.75.82	192.168.75.83

2. Log on to SVR-DC-A, using the domain Administrator account and the password **Pa$$w0rd**. In the left pane of the Server Manager console, click the Local Server icon. The Properties tile appears in the right pane.

Question 1	How did the computer obtain its current IP address? How can you determine this?

3. Click the Ethernet value. The Network Connections dialog box appears.

4. Right-click the Ethernet connection and, from the context menu, select Properties. The Ethernet Properties sheet appears.

5. Double-click Internet Protocol Version 4 (TCP/IPv4). The Internet Protocol Version 4 (TCP/IPv4) Properties sheet appears (see Figure 10-1).

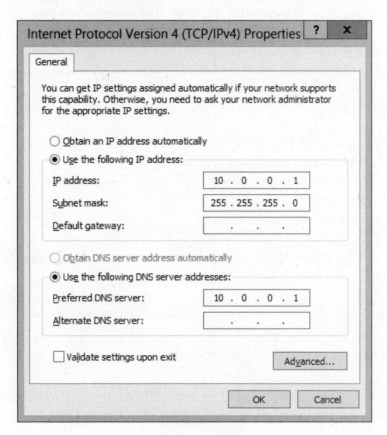

Figure 10-1
The Internet Protocol Version 4 (TCP/IPv4) Properties sheet

6. Select the *Use the following IP address* option and, in the text boxes, type the IP Address, Subnet Mask, and Preferred DNS server address you specified for the SVR-DC-A server in Table 10-5.

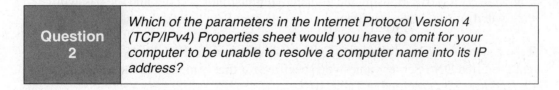

| Question 2 | Which of the parameters in the Internet Protocol Version 4 (TCP/IPv4) Properties sheet would you have to omit for your computer to be unable to resolve a computer name into its IP address? |

7. Click OK to close the Internet Protocol Version 4 (TCP/IPv4) Properties sheet.

8. Double-click Internet Protocol Version 6 (TCP/IPv6). The Internet Protocol Version 6 (TCP/IPv6) Properties sheet appears (see Figure 10-2).

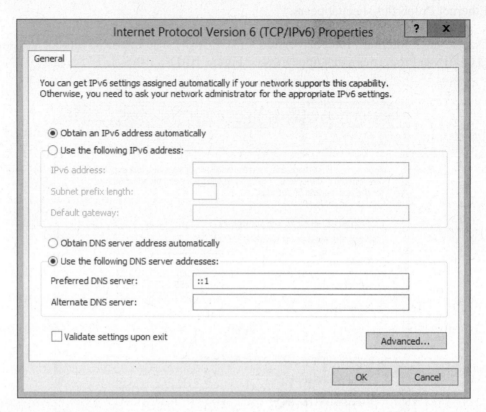

Figure 10-2
The Internet Protocol Version 4 (TCP/IPv4) Properties sheet

9. Select the *Use the following IP address* option and, in the IPv6 address text box, type the IPv6 Address value you specified for the SVR-DC-A server in Table 10-4.

10. In the Subnet prefix length text box, type **64** and click OK to close the Internet Protocol Version 6 (TCP/IPv6) Properties sheet.

11. Click OK to close the Ethernet Properties sheet.

12. Close the Network Connections window.

13. Log on to SVR-MBR-B, using the domain Administrator account and the password **Pa$$w0rd**. When the Server Manager console appears, click the Local Server icon.

14. Repeat steps 3 to 10 and configure SVR-MBR-B to use the IP Address, Subnet Mask, and Preferred DNS Server values you specified for that computer in Table 10-5 and the IPv6 address you specified in Table 10-4.

15. Take a screen shot of the Internet Protocol Version 4 (TCP/IPv4) Properties sheet on SVR-MBR-B by pressing Alt+Prt Scr, and then paste the resulting image into the Lab 10 worksheet file in the page provided by pressing Ctrl+V.

16. Click OK to close the Internet Protocol Version 4 (TCP/IPv4) Properties sheet.

17. Click OK to close the Ethernet Properties sheet.

18. Close the Network Connections window.

End of exercise. You can leave any windows open for the next exercise.

Lab Challenge	Configuring TCP/IP with Windows PowerShell
Overview	In addition to using Server Manager, you can also manually configure TCP/IP on servers using Windows PowerShell.
Completion time	10 minutes

To complete this challenge, you must use Windows PowerShell commands on the SVR-MBR-C server to configure the TCP/IP client to use the IP Address, Subnet Mask, and Preferred DNS Server address you specified for that computer in Table 10-5 and the IPv6 address you calculated in Table 10-4. Write the necessary commands in the Lab 10 worksheet.

End of exercise. You can leave any windows open for the next exercise.

Exercise 10.3	Testing Network Connections
Overview	After manually configuring the three servers' TCP/IP clients, you must test them by trying to connect to the other servers on the network. In this exercise, you use the Ping utility to test the computer's communications capabilities.
Completion time	10 minutes

1. On SVR-MBR-B, right-click the lower left corner of the screen and, from the context menu that appears, select Command Prompt (Admin). An Administrator: Command Prompt window appears.

2. In the Command Prompt window, type **ping 127.0.0.1** and press Enter. The computer successfully pings the specified address.

Question 3	*What does this result prove about the computer's network connectivity?*

Question 4	What would be the result if you unplugged a computer's network cable before executing the ping 127.0.0.1 command?

3. In the Command Prompt window, type **ping svr-dc-a** and press Enter. The computer successfully pings the specified computer.

Question 5	What does the result of this ping test prove?

Question 6	How was the computer able to resolve the name svr-dc-a into its IP address?

4. In the Command Prompt window, type **ping svr-mbr-c** and press Enter. The computer fails to ping the specified computer.

5. On SVR-DC-A, open an Administrator: Command Prompt window and type **ping svr-mbr-b** and press Enter. The computer fails to ping the specified computer.

6. In the Command Prompt window, type **ping svr-mbr-c** and press Enter. The computer fails to ping the specified computer.

Question 7	Why did these three ping tests fail, when the previous tests succeeded?

End of lab.

LAB 11
DEPLOYING AND CONFIGURING THE DHCP SERVICE

THIS LAB CONTAINS THE FOLLOWING EXERCISES AND ACTIVITIES:

Exercise 11.1   Installing the DHCP Server Role

Exercise 11.2   Creating a DHCPv4 Scope

Exercise 11.3   Creating a DHCPv6 Scope

Exercise 11.4   Activating DHCP

Lab Challenge   Confirming DHCP

BEFORE YOU BEGIN

The lab environment consists of computers connected to a local area network, along with a server that functions as the domain controller for a domain called *adatum.com*. The computers required for this lab are listed in Table 11-1.

Table 11-1
Computers Required for Lab 11

Computer	Operating System	Computer Name
Domain controller	Windows Server 2012	SVR-DC-A
Member server	Windows Server 2012	SVR-MBR-B
Member server	Windows Server 2012	SVR-MBR-C

In addition to the computers, you also require the software listed in Table 11-2 to complete Lab 11.

Table 11-2
Software Required for Lab 11

Software	Location
Lab 11 student worksheet	Lab11_worksheet.docx (provided by instructor)

Working with Lab Worksheets

Each lab in this manual requires that you answer questions, shoot screen shots, and perform other activities that you will document in a worksheet named for the lab, such as Lab11_worksheet.docx. It is recommended that you use a USB flash drive to store your worksheets, so you can submit them to your instructor for review. As you perform the exercises in each lab, open the appropriate worksheet file, fill in the required information, and save the file to your flash drive.

After completing this lab, you will be able to:

- Install the DHCP Server role

- Create DHCPv4 and DHCPv6 scopes

- Activate the DHCP client on network servers

- Confirm DHCP IP address assignments

Estimated lab time: 60 minutes

Exercise 11.1	Installing the DHCP Server Role
Overview	In this exercise, you use the Add Roles and Features Wizard to install the DHCP Server role on your network domain controller components to a server running Windows Server 2012.
Mindset	Is your domain controller capable of taking on the additional role of DHCP server? Check your available server resources and consider the number of DHCP clients on your network.
Completion time	10 minutes

1. Log on to the SVR-DC-A computer, which has its Server Manager console open, using the domain Administrator account and the password **Pa$$w0rd**. Select Manage > Add Roles and Features. The Add Roles and Features Wizard appears, displaying the Before you begin page.

2. Click Next. The *Select Installation Type* page appears.

3. Leave the *Role-based or feature-based installation* radio button selected and click Next. The *Select Destination Server* page appears.

4. Click Next to accept the default local server. The *Select Server Roles* page appears.

5. Select the DHCP Server check box. The *Add features that are required for DHCP Server?* page appears.

6. Click Add features.

7. Click Next. The *Select features* page appears.

8. Click Next. The *DHCP Server* page appears.

9. Click Next. The *Confirm installation selections* page appears.

10. Click Install. The *Installation progress* page appears as the wizard installs the selected roles and features (see Figure 11-1).

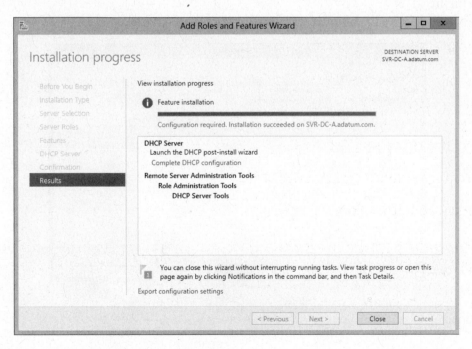

Figure 11-1
The *Installation progress* page of the DHCP installation

11. Click *Complete DHCP Configuration*. The DHCP Post-Install Configuration Wizard appears, displaying the Description page.

12. Click Next. The Authorization page appears.

13. Click Commit to use the default Authorization settings. The Summary page appears.

14. Click Close. The DHCP Post-Install Configuration Wizard closes.

15. Click Close. The Add Roles and Features Wizard closes.

End of exercise. Close any open windows before you begin the next exercise.

Exercise 11.2	Creating a DHCPv4 Scope
Overview	A scope is a range of IP addresses that a DHCP server uses to supply clients on a particular subnet with IP addresses. In this exercise, you create a scope for IPv4 addresses on your DHCP server.
Mindset	What IPv4 addressing policies does your organization have in place?
Completion time	15 minutes

1. On SVR-DC-A, in Server Manager, click Tools > DHCP. The DHCP console appears (see Figure 11-2).

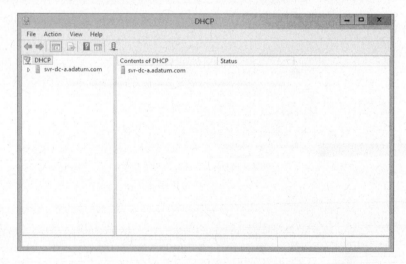

Figure 11-2
The DHCP console

2. Expand the svr-dc-a.adatum.com node.

3. Expand and right-click the IPv4 node and, from the context menu, select New Scope. The New Scope Wizard appears.

4. Click Next to bypass the Welcome page. The Scope Name page appears.

5. In the Name text box, type **10.0.0.0** and click Next. The IP Address Range page appears.

6. In the Start IP address text box, type **10.0.0.1**.

7. In the End IP address text box, type **10.0.0.100**.

Question 1	Notice that the wizard automatically adds a value to the Subnet mask text box. Where did this value come from?

8. In the *Subnet mask* text box, key **255.255.255.0**. Then click Next. The *Add Exclusions and Delay* page appears.

9. In the *Start IP address* text box, type **10.0.0.1**.

10. In the *End IP address* text box, type **10.0.0.10**.

11. Click Add. The address appears in the *Excluded address range* list.

Question 2	Why is it necessary to exclude addresses from the range of addresses included in the scope?

Question 3	How would it be possible to leave the 10.0.0.1 address as part of the scope and still use it for the DHCP server?

12. Click *Next*. The *Lease Duration* page appears.

13. Click Next to accept the default value. The *Configure DHCP Options* page appears.

14. Click Next to accept the *Yes, I want to configure these options now* option. The *Router (Default Gateway)* page appears.

15. In the IP address text box, key **10.0.0.1** and then click Add.

16. Click Next to continue. The *Domain Name and DNS Servers* page appears.

17. Click Next. The *WINS Servers* page appears.

18. Click Next to bypass the page. The *Activate Scope* page appears.

19. Click Next to accept the default *Yes, I want to activate this scope now* option. The *Completing the New Scope Wizard* page appears.

20. Click Finish. The scope is added to the console.

21. Expand the IPv4 node and the new scope, and then select the Address Pool folder.

22. Take a screen shot of the DHCP console, showing the contents of the Address Pool folder, by pressing Alt+Prt Scr, and then paste the resulting image into the Lab 11 worksheet file in the page provided by pressing Ctrl+V.

End of exercise. You can leave the windows open for the next exercise.

Exercise 11.3	Creating a DHCPv6 Scope
Overview	In this exercise, you create a DHCP scope to allocate IPv6 addresses to the computers on your network.
Mindset	What IPv6 addressing policies does your organization have in place?
Completion time	15 minutes

1. On SVR-DC-A, in the DHCP console, expand and right-click the IPv6 node and, from the context menu, select New Scope. The New Scope Wizard for IPv6 addresses appears, displaying the Welcome page.

2. Click Next. The *Scope Name* page appears.

3. In the Name text box, type **IPv6**. Then click Next. The Scope Prefix page appears (see Figure 11-3).

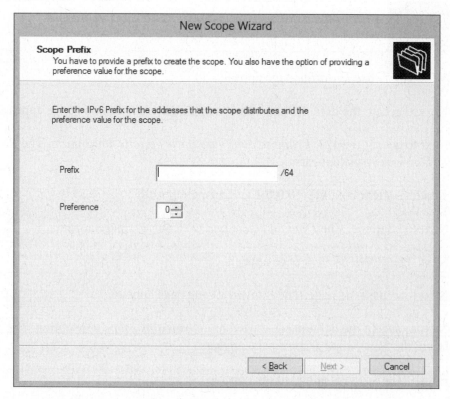

Figure 11-3
The Scope Prefix page in the New Scope Wizard

4. In the Prefix text box, type **fd00::** and click Next. The *Add Exclusions* page appears.

5. In the *Start IPv6 address* text box, type **0:0:0:1** and click Add. The address appears in the *Excluded address range* list.

6. Click Next. The *Scope Lease* page appears.

7. Click Next. The *Completing the New Scope Wizard* page appears.

8. Click Finish. The wizard creates the scope.

9. Expand the Scope [fd00:] IPv6 node you just created.

10. Click the Scope Options node, then right-click it, and, from the context menu, select Configure Options. The Scope Options dialog box appears.

11. Select the check box for the *DNS Recursive Name Server IPv6 Address List* option.

12. In the *New IPv6 address* text box, type **fd00::0:0:0:1** and click Add. Wait for DNS Validation to complete. The address appears in the *Current IPv6 address* list.

Question 4	*Where did the fd00::0:0:0:1 address that you supplied for the DNS Recursive Name Server IPv6 Address List option come from?*

13. Take a screen shot of the Scope Options dialog box, showing the option you just configured, by pressing Alt+Prt Scr, and then paste the resulting image into the Lab 11 worksheet file in the page provided by pressing Ctrl+V.

14. Click OK to close the Scope Options dialog box.

End of exercise. You can leave the windows open for the next exercise.

Exercise 11.4	Activating DHCP
Overview	In this exercise, you activate the DHCP clients on your network.
Mindset	How do you activate the DHCP clients on a server running Windows Server 2012?
Completion time	10 minutes

1. Log on to the SVR-MBR-B computer, using the domain Administrator account and the password **Pa$$w0rd**. Launch Server Manager and, in the left pane, click the Local Server icon.

2. In the Properties tile, click the Ethernet setting. The Network Connections window appears.

3. Right-click the Ethernet icon and, from the context menu, select Properties. The Ethernet Properties sheet appears.

4. Double-click Internet Protocol Version 4 (TCP/IPv4). The Internet Protocol Version 4 (TCP/IPv4) Properties sheet appears.

5. Select the *Obtain an IP address automatically* option and the *Obtain DNS server address automatically* option. Then click OK.

6. Double-click Internet Protocol Version 6 (TCP/IPv6). The Internet Protocol Version 6 (TCP/IPv6) Properties sheet appears (see Figure 11-4).

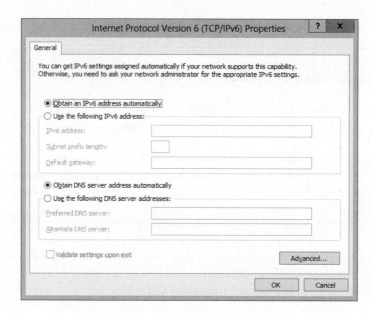

Figure 11-4
The Internet Protocol Version 6 (TCP/IPv6) Properties sheet

7. Make sure that the *Obtain an IPv6 address automatically* and *Obtain DNS server address automatically* options are selected. Then click OK.

8. Click OK to close the Ethernet Properties sheet.

9. Close the Network Connections window.

10. Restart the SVR-MBR-B computer.

11. Log on to the SVR-MBR-C computer, using the domain Administrator account and the password **Pa$$w0rd**. Repeat steps 1 to 10 to enable the DHCPv4 and DHCPv6 clients and restart the computer.

End of exercise. You can leave the windows open for the next exercise.

Lab Challenge	Confirming DHCP
Overview	To complete this challenge, you must demonstrate that the SVR-MBR-B and SVR-MBR-C computers have both obtained IPv4 and IPv6 addresses from the DHCP server running on SVR-DC-A.
Completion time	10 minutes

Take screen shots of the SVR-MBR-B and SVR-MBR-C computers, showing the addresses they have obtained through DHCP, by pressing Alt+Prt Scr, and then paste the resulting images into the Lab 11 worksheet file in the page provided by pressing Ctrl+V.

End of lab.

LAB 12
DEPLOYING AND CONFIGURING THE DNS SERVICE

THIS LAB CONTAINS THE FOLLOWING EXERCISES AND ACTIVITIES:

Exercise 12.1	Designing a DNS Namespace
Lab Challenge	Remote DNS Administration
Exercise 12.2	Creating a DNS Zone
Exercise 12.3	Creating DNS Domains
Exercise 12.4	Creating DNS Resource Records
Lab Challenge	Using Reverse Name Resolution

BEFORE YOU BEGIN

The lab environment consists of computers connected to a local area network, along with a server that functions as the domain controller for a domain called *adatum.com*. The computers required for this lab are listed in Table 12-1.

Table 12-1
Computers Required for Lab 12

Computer	Operating System	Computer Name
Domain controller	Windows Server 2012	SVR-DC-A
Member server	Windows Server 2012	SVR-MBR-B
Member server	Windows Server 2012	SVR-MBR-C

In addition to the computers, you also require the software listed in Table 12-2 to complete Lab 12.

Table 12-2
Software Required for Lab 12

Software	Location
Lab 12 student worksheet	Lab12_worksheet.docx (provided by instructor)

Working with Lab Worksheets

Each lab in this manual requires that you answer questions, take screen shots, and perform other activities that you will document in a worksheet named for the lab, such as Lab12_worksheet.docx. It is recommended that you use a USB flash drive to store your worksheets, so you can submit them to your instructor for review. As you perform the exercises in each lab, open the appropriate worksheet file, fill in the required information, and save the file to your flash drive.

After completing this lab, you will be able to:

- Design a DNS namespace

- Configure remote DNS administration

- Create and manage DNS zones, domains, and resource records

- Configure reverse name resolution

Estimated lab time: 90 minutes

Exercise 12.1	Designing a DNS Namespace
Overview	Your firm is launching a new division, which will have its own DNS namespace, and your first task is to design that namespace by specifying appropriate domain and host names for the computers in the division.
Mindset	Why is it practical and necessary to have a policy in place for the naming of your organization's domains and hosts?
Completion time	20 minutes

1. Design a DNS namespace for your organization that conforms to the following guidelines.

   - The root domain name for the organization is **adatum.com**. All of the additional domains you create must be subordinate to this domain.

   - The internal network must be in a different domain from the external network.

   - The organization consists of three internal divisions: Sales, Human Resources, and Production. Each division must be represented by a separate subdomain in the namespace.

   - Each division has departmental servers performing various roles and as many as 200 workstations, only some of which are shown in the diagram. Your host names should identify the function of each computer.

   - Three servers on an external perimeter network host the company's Internet services: Web, FTP, and e-mail. These servers must be in the domain adatum.com.

2. On the worksheet shown in Figure 12-1 and in your Lab 12 worksheet file, write the domain names and the fully qualified domain names you have selected for the computers in the appropriate spaces.

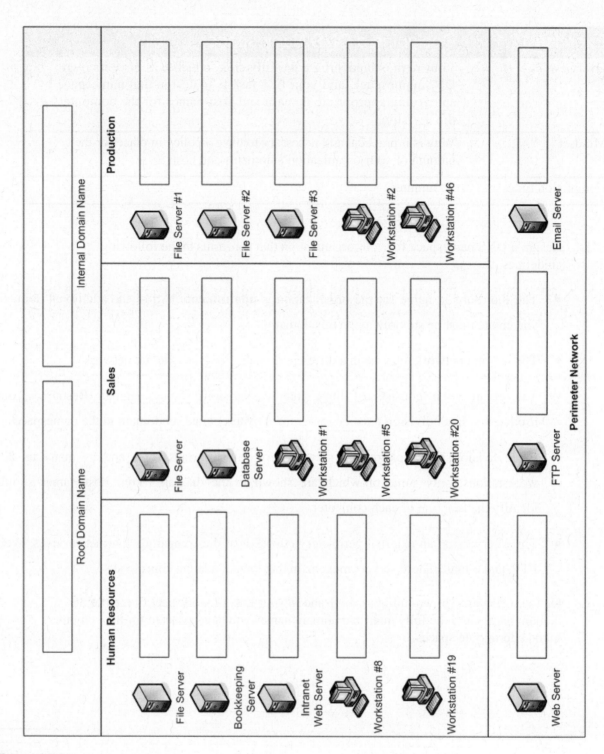

Figure 12-1
DNS Namespace Design Worksheet

End of exercise.

Lab Challenge	Remote DNS Administration
Overview	To complete this challenge, you must configure SVR-MBR-C to manage the DNS server running on SVR-DC-A using the DNS console.
Completion time	10 minutes

List the steps you took to configure SVR-MBR-C and take a screen shot of the Connect to DNS Server dialog box, by pressing Alt+Prt Scr, and then paste the resulting images into the Lab 12 worksheet file in the page provided by pressing Ctrl+V.

End of exercise. You can leave the windows open for the next exercise.

Exercise 12.2	Creating a DNS Zone
Overview	The zone is the administrative division that DNS servers use to separate domains. The first step in implementing the DNS namespace you designed is to create a zone representing your root domain.
Mindset	What is the relationship between DNS zones and DNS domains?
Completion time	10 minutes

1. Log on to the SVR-MBR-C computer, using the domain Administrator account and the password **Pa$$w0rd.** In Server Manager, click Tools > DNS. The DNS Manager console appears.

2. Expand the SVR-DC-A node and select the Forward Lookup Zones folder (see Figure 12-2).

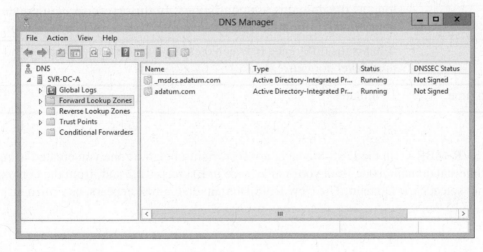

Figure 12-2
The DNS Manager console

Question 1	*Why is a zone for the root domain of your DNS namespace already present in the Forward Lookup Zones folder?*

3. Right-click the Forward Lookup Zones folder and, from the context menu, select New Zone. The New Zone Wizard appears.

4. Click Next to bypass the Welcome page. The *Zone Type* page appears.

5. Leave the *Primary Zone* option and the *Store the zone in Active Directory* check box selected and click Next. The *Active Directory Zone Replication Scope* page appears.

6. Click Next to accept the default setting. The *Zone Name* page appears.

7. In the *Zone name* text box, type the internal domain name from the diagram you created in Exercise 12.1 and click *Next*. The *Dynamic Update* page appears.

8. Select the *Allow both nonsecure and secure dynamic updates* option and click Next. The *Completing the New Zone Wizard* page appears.

9. Click Finish. The new zone appears in the Forward Lookup Zones folder in the console.

Question 2	*What resource records appear in the new zone you created by default?*

End of exercise. You can leave the windows open for the next exercise.

Exercise 12.3	Creating DNS Domains
Overview	A single zone on a DNS server can encompass multiple domains, as long as the domains are contiguous. In this exercise, you create the departmental domains you specified in your namespace design.
Mindset	What is the difference between creating a second-level domain and a third-level domain?
Completion time	10 minutes

1. On SVR-MBR-C, in the DNS Manager console, right-click the zone you created using the internal domain name from your namespace in Exercise 12.2 and, from the context menu, select New Domain. The New DNS Domain dialog box appears, as shown in Figure 12-3.

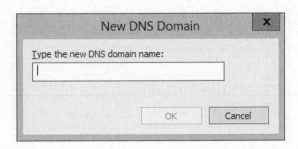

Figure 12-3
The New DNS Domain dialog box

2. In the *Type the new DNS domain name* text box, type the name of the Human Resources domain you specified in your namespace design and click OK.

> **NOTE**
>
> *When you create a domain within a zone, you specify the name for the new domain relative to the zone name. For example, to create the hr.int.contoso.com domain in the int.contoso.com zone, you would specify only the hr name in the New DNS Domain dialog box.*

3. Repeat steps 1 to 2 to create the domains for the Sales and Production departments from your namespace design.

> **Question 3** | *What resource records appear in the new domains you created by default?*

End of exercise. You can leave the windows open for the next exercise.

Exercise 12.4	Creating DNS Resource Records
Overview	Now that you have created the zones and domains for your namespace, you can begin to populate them with the resource records that the DNS server uses to resolve host names into IP addresses.
Mindset	What good are zones and domains without resource records?
Completion time	20 minutes

1. On SVR-MBR-C, in the DNS Manager console, expand and right-click your root domain zone (adatum.com) and, from the context menu, select New Host (A or AAAA). The New Host dialog box appears, as shown in Figure 12-4.

Figure 12-4
The New Host dialog box

2. In the Name text box, type the host name of the Internet web server you specified in your namespace design.

3. In the IP Address text box, type **10.0.0.10**.

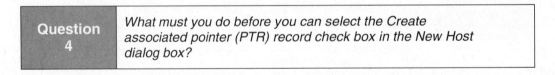

Question 4	What must you do before you can select the Create associated pointer (PTR) record check box in the New Host dialog box?

4. Click Add Host. A DNS message box appears, stating that the resource record was created.

5. Click OK. A new, blank Add Host dialog box appears.

6. Repeat steps 2 to 4 to create Host records for the Internet FTP and Internet e-mail servers in your namespace design, using the IP addresses 10.0.0.11 and 10.0.0.12, respectively.

7. In the three domains you created in Exercise 12.3, create Host resource records for all of the remaining computers in your namespace design, placing each computer within its appropriate subdomain; Human Resources, Sales, or Production, using the names you specified in your diagram and different IP addresses in the 10.0.0.10 to 10.0.0.30 range.

NOTE	For the purposes of this exercise, the actual IP addresses you use when creating your resource records do not matter. In an actual DNS deployment, you must either specify an appropriate IP address for each host, based on the subnet to which the computer is connected, or rely on DHCP to create the resource records for the computers.

8. Click Done to close the Add Host dialog box.

9. Take a screen shot of the DNS Manager console, showing the resource records you created in the Human Resources domain, by pressing Alt+Prt Scr, and then paste the resulting image into the Lab 12 worksheet file in the page provided by pressing Ctrl+V.

10. Close the DNS Manager console.

End of exercise. You can leave the windows open for the next exercise.

Lab Challenge	Using Reverse Name Resolution
Overview	Reverse name resolution is when a resolver sends an IP address to a DNS server and receives a host name in return, rather than sending a host name and receiving an IP address.
Completion time	20 minutes

To complete this challenge, you must configure the DNS server on SVR-DC-A to perform reverse name resolutions for all of the resource records you created in Exercise 12.4.

List the basic tasks you performed to complete the challenge and then take a screen shot of the DNS Manager console, showing the elements you created during the challenge, by pressing Alt+Prt Scr, and then paste the resulting image into the Lab 12 worksheet file in the page provided by pressing Ctrl+V.

End of lab.

LAB 13
INSTALLING DOMAIN CONTROLLERS

THIS LAB CONTAINS THE FOLLOWING EXERCISES AND ACTIVITIES: _ _ _ _

Exercise 13.1   Installing Active Directory Domain Services Role

Exercise 13.2   Creating a New Forest

Exercise 13.3   Creating a Child Domain

Lab Challenge   Installing AD DS on Server Core

BEFORE YOU BEGIN

The lab environment consists of three servers connected to a local area network, which you will configure to function as the domain controller for a domain called *adatum.com*. The computers required for this lab are listed in Table 13-1.

Table 13-1
Computers Required for Lab 13

Computer	Operating System	Computer Name
Domain controller 1	Windows Server 2012	SVR-DC-A
Domain Controller 2	Windows Server 2012	SVR-DC-B
Domain controller 3	Windows Server 2012	SVR-DC-C

In addition to the computers, you also require the software listed in Table 13-2 to complete Lab 13.

Table 13-2
Software Required for Lab 13

Software	Location
Lab 13 student worksheet	Lab13_worksheet.docx (provided by instructor)

Working with Lab Worksheets

Each lab in this manual requires that you answer questions, take screen shots, and perform other activities that you will document in a worksheet named for the lab, such as Lab13_worksheet.docx. It is recommended that you use a USB flash drive to store your worksheets, so you can submit them to your instructor for review. As you perform the exercises in each lab, open the appropriate worksheet file, fill in the required information, and save the file to your flash drive.

After completing this lab, you will be able to:

- Install the Active Directory Domain Services role

- Create a new AD DS forest

- Create a new subdomain

- Promote a domain controller using Server Core

Estimated lab time: 55 minutes

Exercise 13.1	Installing the Active Directory Domain Services Role
Overview	In this exercise, you use the Add Roles and Features Wizard to install the Active Directory Domain Services role on a newly installed server running Windows Server 2012.
Mindset	What are the minimum requirements for a domain controller server? Does this server fulfill them?
Completion time	10 minutes

1. Log on to the SVR-DC-A computer, using the local Administrator account and the password **Pa$$w0rd**. When the Server Manager console appears, select Manage > Add Roles and Features. The Add Roles and Features Wizard appears, displaying the *Before you begin* page.

2. Click Next. The *Select Installation Type* page appears.

3. Leave the *Role-based or feature-based installation* radio button selected and click Next. The *Select Destination Server* page appears.

4. Click Next to accept the default local server. The *Select Server Roles* page appears.

5. Select the Active Directory Domain Services check box. The *Add features that are required for Active Directory Domain Services?* page appears.

6. Click *Add features*.

7. Click Next. The *Select features* page appears.

8. Click Next. The *Active Directory Domain Services* page appears.

9. Click Next. The *Confirm installation selections* page appears.

10. Click Install. The *Installation progress* page appears as the wizard installs the selected roles and features (see Figure 13-1).

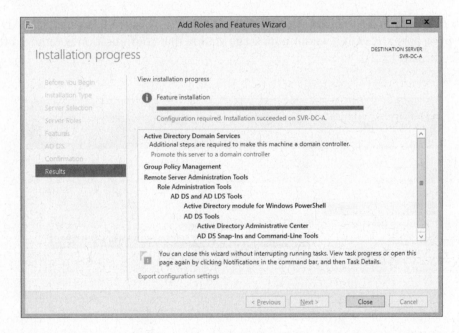

Figure 13-1
The *Installation progress* page of the Add Roles and Features Wizard

11. Click Close. The Add Roles and Features Wizard closes.

12. In Server Manager, click Tools> Active Directory Users and Computers. The Active Directory Users and Computers console fails to open properly.

Question 1	Why can't you open the Active Directory Users and Computers console properly at this time?

End of exercise. You can leave any windows open for the next exercise.

Exercise 13.2	Creating a New Forest
Overview	Once you have installed the Active Directory Domain Services role, you must promote the server to a domain controller. In this exercise, you create a new domain in a new forest and configure the server to function as the domain controller for that domain.
Mindset	What are the functions performed by the first domain controller in an AD DS forest?
Completion time	15 minutes

1. On SVR-DC-A, in Server Manager, click the AD DS link in the left pane. The AD DS home page appears, with a warning message stating that configuration is required for AD DS (see Figure 13-2).

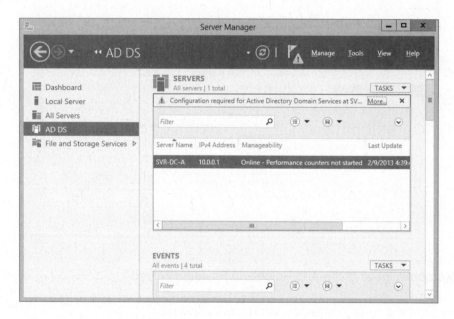

Figure 13-2
The AD DS home page

2. Click the More link. The All Servers Task Details window appears (see Figure 13-3).

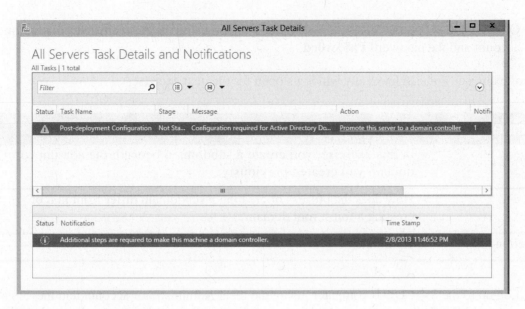

Figure 13-3
The All Servers Task Details window

3. Click the *Promote this server to a domain controller* link. The Active Directory Domain Services Configuration Wizard appears, displaying the *Deployment Configuration* page.

4. Select the *Add a new forest* option, and in the *Root domain name* text box, type **adatum.com** and click Next. The *Domain Controller Options* page appears.

5. In the Password and Confirm Password text boxes, type **Pa$$w0rd** and click Next. The *DNS Options* page appears.

6. Click Next. The *Additional Options* page appears and, after a brief delay, the NetBIOS domain name appears in the text box.

7. Click Next. The *Paths* page appears.

8. Click Next. The *Review Options* page appears.

9. Click the View Script button. A Notepad window appears, containing a Windows PowerShell script equivalent to the settings you just configured in the wizard.

10. Take a screen shot of the Notepad window, showing the Windows PowerShell script the wizard created, by pressing Alt+Prt Scr, and then paste the resulting image into the Lab 13 worksheet file in the page provided by pressing Ctrl+V.

11. Close the Notepad window without saving the file and click Next. The *Prerequisites check* page appears. The wizard performs the necessary checks, and a notice appears on the page, indicating that all prerequisite checks have passed successfully.

12. Click Install. The *Installation* page appears as the wizard creates the new forest and promotes the server to a domain controller. After several minutes, the computer restarts.

13. On SVR-DC-A, press CTRL+ALT+DEL and log on using the **Adatum\Administrator** account and the password **Pa$$w0rd**.

End of exercise. You can leave any windows open for the next exercise.

Exercise 13.3	Creating a Child Domain
Overview	In this exercise, you create a subdomain beneath the adatum.com domain you created previously.
Mindset	How does the process of creating a subdomain differ from that of creating a forest root domain?
Completion time	15 minutes

1. Log on to the SVR-DC-B computer, using the local Administrator account and the password **Pa$$w0rd**. In Server Manager, use the Add Roles and Features Wizard to install the Active Directory Domain Services role, as you did in Exercise 13.1.

2. On the *Installation progress* page that appears at the end of the Active Directory Domain Services role installation procedure, click the *Promote this server to a domain controller* hyperlink. The Active Directory Domain Services Configuration Wizard appears, displaying the *Deployment Configuration* page.

3. Select the *Add a new domain to an existing forest* option and, in the *Select domain type* drop-down list, leave *Child Domain* selected.

Question 2	What would the difference in results be if you were to choose the Tree Domain option rather than the Child Domain option?

Question 3	By default, the wizard configures this domain controller to function as a DNS server. Under what circumstances would it be practical not to configure this domain controller to be a DNS server?

4. Click Select. A *Credentials for deployment operation* dialog box appears.

5. In the User name text box, type **ADATUM\Administrator**, and in the Password text box, type **Pa$$w0rd** and click OK. A *Select a domain from the forest* dialog box appears.

6. Select adatum.com and click OK. The domain name appears in the *Parent domain name* field of the *Deployment Configuration* page.

7. In the *New domain name* text box, type **NY** and click Next. The *Domain Controller Options* page appears.

Question 4	*Why does the Domain Controller Options page have a* Domain functional level *drop-down menu, but not a* Forest functional level *drop-down menu?*

8. In the Password and Confirm Password text boxes, type **Pa$$w0rd** and click Next. The *DNS Options* page appears.

9. Click Next. The *Additional Options* page appears and, after a brief delay, the NetBIOS domain name appears in the text box.

10. Click Next. The *Paths* page appears.

11. Click Next. The *Review Options* page appears.

12. Take a screen shot of the Review Options page by pressing Alt+Prt Scr, and then paste the resulting image into the Lab 13 worksheet file in the page provided by pressing Ctrl+V.

13. Click Next. The *Prerequisites Check* page appears.

14. After the system passes all the prerequisite checks, click Install. The wizard creates the new domain and configures the server to function as a domain controller.

End of exercise. Close any open windows before you begin the next exercise.

Lab Challenge	Installing AD DS on Server Core
Overview	In this exercise, you configure a server to function as a domain controller using the Server Core interface.
Completion time	20 minutes

1. On SVR-DC-C, Windows Server 2012 has been installed using the Server Core option.

2. To complete this challenge, you must configure the server to function as a replica domain controller for the adatum.com domain using only Windows PowerShell commands. After the new Domain Controller reboots, press Ctrl+Alt+Del.

    Write out the necessary commands, using all the required parameters and the correct syntax. Then, take a screen shot of the Login Prompt page, showing that the server is now a domain controller, by pressing Alt+Prt Scr, and then pasting the resulting image into the Lab 13 worksheet file in the page provided by pressing Ctrl+V.

    At the Command Prompt, type **powershell** to execute Windows PowerShell, as you'll be using Windows PowerShell commands.

End of lab.

LAB 14
CREATING AND MANAGING ACTIVE DIRECTORY USERS AND COMPUTERS

THIS LAB CONTAINS THE FOLLOWING EXERCISES AND ACTIVITIES: _ _ _ _

Exercise 14.1	Creating Computer Objects
Exercise 14.2	Creating a Single User
Exercise 14.3	Using Active Directory Administrative Center
Lab Challenge	Creating Users with Windows PowerShell
Lab Challenge	Creating Multiple Users with LDIFDE

BEFORE YOU BEGIN

The lab environment consists of three servers connected to a local area network, which you will configure to function as the domain controller for a domain called *adatum.com*. The computers required for this lab are listed in Table 14-1.

Table 14-1
Computers Required for Lab 14

Computer	Operating System	Computer Name
Domain controller 1	Windows Server 2012	SVR-DC-A
Member server 2	Windows Server 2012	SVR-MBR-B
Member server 3	Windows Server 2012	SVR-MBR-C

In addition to the computers, you also require the software listed in Table 14-2 to complete Lab 14.

Table 14-2
Software Required for Lab 14

Software	Location
Lab 14 student worksheet	Lab14_worksheet.docx (provided by instructor)

Working with Lab Worksheets

Each lab in this manual requires that you answer questions, shoot screen shots, and perform other activities that you will document in a worksheet named for the lab, such as Lab14_worksheet.docx. It is recommended that you use a USB flash drive to store your worksheets, so you can submit them to your instructor for review. As you perform the exercises in each lab, open the appropriate worksheet file, fill in the required information, and save the file to your flash drive.

After completing this lab, you will be able to:

- Create AD DS computer objects

- Create AD DS user objects

- Create objects using Windows PowerShell

- Create multiple objects using LDIFDE

Estimated lab time: 55 minutes

Exercise 14.1	Creating Computer Objects
Overview	In this exercise, you use the Active Directory Users and Computers console on a newly installed domain controller to create a computer object.
Mindset	Is it always necessary to create computer objects manually?
Completion time	10 minutes

1.   Log on to the SVR-DC-A computer, which has the Server Manager console open, using the domain Administrator account and the password **Pa$$w0rd**. Select Tools > Active Directory Users and Computers. The *Active Directory Users and Computers* console appears.

2.   In the left pane, expand the adatum.com node, if needed, and select the Computers container.

3.   Right-click the Computers container and, from the context menu, click New > Computer. The New Object – Computer Wizard appears (see Figure 14-1).

Figure 14-1
The New Object—Computer Wizard

4.   In the *Computer name* text box, type **Wkstn1**.

5.   Under *User or group*, click Change. The Select User or Group dialog box appears.

6.   In the *Enter the object name to select* text box, type **Domain Computers** and click OK. The group appears in the *User or group* text box.

7.   Click OK. The wizard creates the computer object.

8.   Take a screen shot of the Computers container in the Active Directory Users and Computers console, showing the computer object the wizard created, by pressing Alt+Prt Scr, and then paste the resulting image into the Lab 14 worksheet file in the page provided by pressing Ctrl+V.

End of exercise. You can leave the windows open for the next exercise.

Exercise 14.2	Creating a Single User
Overview	In this exercise, you use the Active Directory Users and Computers console on a newly installed domain controller to create a domain user account.
Mindset	How many other ways are there to create a user object?
Completion time	10 minutes

1. On the SVR-DC-A computer, in the Active Directory Users and Computers console, select the People organizational unit.

2. From the Action menu, select New > User. The New Object – User Wizard appears (see Figure 14-2).

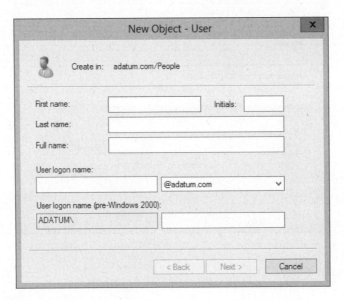

Figure 14-2
The New Object—User Wizard

3. In the *First name* text box, type **Lori** and in the *Last name* text box, type **Kane**.

4. In the *User logon name* text box, type **lkane** and click Next. The second page of the New Object – User Wizard appears.

5. In the Password and Confirm password fields, type **Pa$$w0rd**.

6. Clear the *User must change password at next logon* check box and click Next. A confirmation page listing the settings you configured appears.

7. Click Finish. The wizard creates the user object and closes.

8. Take a screen shot of the People container in the Active Directory Users and Computers console, showing the user object the wizard created, by pressing Alt+Prt Scr, and then paste the resulting image into the Lab 14 worksheet file in the page provided by pressing Ctrl+V.

End of exercise. Close any open windows before you begin the next exercise.

Exercise 14.3	Using Active Directory Administrative Center
Overview	In this exercise, you use the Active Directory Administrative Center console to create user and computer objects.
Mindset	What can Active Directory Administrative Center do that other tools cannot?
Completion time	10 minutes

1. On the SVR-DC-A computer, in the Server Manager console, select Tools > Active Directory Administrative Center. The *Active Directory Administrative Center* console appears.

2. In the left pane, select the adatum (local) node and, in the center pane, double-click the Computers container. The contents of the Computers container appears in the center pane.

3. In the right pane, select New > Computer. The Create Computer dialog box appears (see Figure 14-3).

Figure 14-3
The Create Computer dialog box

4. In the *Computer name* text box, type **Wkstn8**.

5. Under Member of, click Add. The Select Groups dialog box appears.

6. In the *Enter the object name to select* box, type **Domain Computers** and click OK. The group appears in the *Member Of* text box.

7. Click OK. The new object appears in the Computers container.

8. Take a screen shot of the Computers container by pressing Alt+Prt Scr, and then paste the resulting image into the Lab 14 worksheet file in the page provided by pressing Ctrl+V.

9. In the left pane, select the adatum (local) node and, in the center pane, double-click the People OU. The contents of the People container appears in the center pane.

10. In the right pane, select New > User. The Create User dialog box appears (see Figure 14-4).

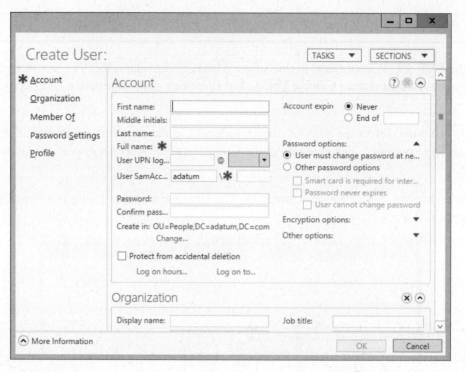

Figure 14-4
The Create User dialog box

11. In the *First name* text box, type **Monica**, and in the *Last name* text box, type **Brink**.

12. In the *User SamAccountName Logon* text box, type **mbrink**. In the Password and Confirm password fields, type **Pa$$w0rd**.

13. Scroll down and, in the *Member of* section, click Add. The *Select Groups* dialog box appears.

14. In the *Enter the object name to select* text box, type **Domain Users** and click OK. The group appears in the *Member Of* text box.

15. Click OK. The new user object appears in the People OU.

16. Take a screen shot of the People by pressing Alt+Prt Scr, and then paste the resulting image into the Lab 14 worksheet file in the page provided by pressing Ctrl+V.

End of exercise. Close any open windows before you begin the next exercise.

Lab Challenge	Creating Users with Windows PowerShell
Overview	You can create Active Directory user objects on a domain controller using Windows PowerShell commands.
Completion time	15 minutes

To complete this challenge, you must use Windows PowerShell commands (and Windows PowerShell commands only) on SVR-DC-A to create user objects in the adatum.com domain, in the People container, for the following users:

- Syed Abbas

- Brenda Diaz

- Steve Masters

For each user, form the user logon name with the person's first initial and surname. Disable the *User must change password at next logon* option and enable the *Password never expires* option.

End of exercise. Close any open windows before you begin the next exercise.

Lab Challenge	Creating Multiple Users Using LDIFDE
Overview	To create batches of users in one operation, you can use the LDIFDE.exe program from the command prompt.
Completion time	15 minutes

To complete this challenge, create a correctly formatted LDIF input data file to create the following domain user accounts in the People OU of the adatum.com domain. For each user, form the user logon name with the person's first initial and surname. For the user principal name, use an e-mail address formed from the user logon name and the domain name.

- Oliver Kiel

- Marie Dubois

- Maurice Taylor

- Esther Valle

- Raffaella Bonaldi

End of lab.

LAB 15
CREATING AND MANAGING ACTIVE DIRECTORY GROUPS AND ORGANIZATIONAL UNITS

THIS LAB CONTAINS THE FOLLOWING EXERCISES AND ACTIVITIES:

Exercise 15.1	Creating Organizational Units
Exercise 15.2	Creating Domain Local Groups
Exercise 15.3	Creating Global Groups
Lab Challenge	Nesting Groups
Exercise 15.4	Delegating Administration

BEFORE YOU BEGIN

The lab environment consists of three servers connected to a local area network, which you will configure to function as the domain controller for a domain called *adatum.com*. The computers required for this lab are listed in Table 15-1.

Table 15-1
Computers Required for Lab 15

Computer	Operating System	Computer Name
Domain controller 1	Windows Server 2012	SVR-DC-A
Member server 2	Windows Server 2012	SVR-MBR-B
Member server 3	Windows Server 2012	SVR-MBR-C

In addition to the computers, you also require the software listed in Table 15-2 to complete Lab 15.

Table 15-2
Software Required for Lab 15

Software	Location
Lab 15 student worksheet	Lab15_worksheet.docx (provided by instructor)

Working with Lab Worksheets

Each lab in this manual requires that you answer questions, take screen shots, and perform other activities that you will document in a worksheet named for the lab, such as Lab15_worksheet.docx. It is recommended that you use a USB flash drive to store your worksheets, so you can submit them to your instructor for review. As you perform the exercises in each lab, open the appropriate worksheet file, fill in the required information, and save the file to your flash drive.

After completing this lab, you will be able to:

- Create AD DS organizational unit objects

- Create AD DS group objects

- Nest groups

- Delegate authority over OUs

Estimated lab time: 55 minutes

Exercise 15.1	Creating Organizational Units
Overview	In this exercise, you create new organizational units in the adatum.com domain, named for the cities in which your company has offices.
Mindset	Under what conditions is it necessary to create a new organizational unit?
Completion time	10 minutes

1. Log on to the SVR-DC-A computer, which has the Server Manager console open, using the domain Administrator account and the password **Pa$$w0rd**. Select Tools > Active Directory Users and Computers. The *Active Directory Users and Computers* console appears.

2. In the left pane, expand the adatum.com node.

3. Right-click the adatum.com node and, from the context menu, click New > Organizational Unit. The New Object – Organizational Unit Wizard appears (see Figure 15-1).

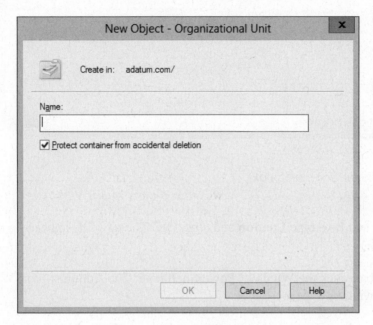

Figure 15-1
The New Object—Organizational Unit Wizard

4. In the Name text box, type **Rome**.

5. Click OK. The wizard creates the Rome OU object.

6. In Server Manager, click Tools > Active Directory Administrative Center. The Active Directory Administrative Center console appears.

7. In the left pane, select the adatum (local) node and, in the right pane under Tasks, select New > Organizational Unit. The Create Organizational Unit dialog box appears (see Figure 15-2).

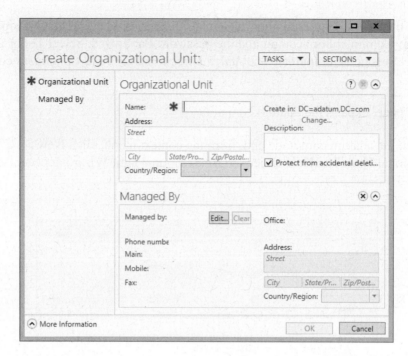

Figure 15-2
The Create Organizational Unit dialog box

8. In the Name text box, type **London** and click OK. The new OU appears in the center pane.

9. On the Taskbar, click the Windows PowerShell icon. The Administrator: Windows PowerShell window appears.

10. At the command prompt, type **New-ADOrganizationalUnit –Name Paris** and press Enter.

Question 1	*What must you do to assign the same Group Policy settings to the systems in all three of the OUs you just created?*

11. In the Active Directory Users and Computers console, press F5 to refresh the console until the Paris OU appears.

12. Take a screen shot of the adatum.com domain in the Active Directory Users and Computers console, showing the OU objects you created, by pressing Alt+Prt Scr, and then paste the resulting image into the Lab 15 worksheet file in the page provided by pressing Ctrl+V.

End of exercise. You can leave the windows open for the next exercise.

Exercise 15.2	Creating Domain Local Groups
Overview	In this exercise, you create domain local groups using the Active Directory Users and Computers console.
Mindset	What is the function of the domain local groups in a group nesting arrangement?
Completion time	10 minutes

1. On the SVR-DC-A computer, in the *Active Directory Users and Computers* console, select the Rome OU you created in Exercise 15.1.

2. Right-click the Rome OU and, from the context menu, click New > Group. The New Object - Group dialog box appears (see Figure 15-3).

Figure 15-3
The New Object—Group dialog box

3. In the Group name text box, type **Rome Backup**.

4. Under *Group scope*, select the *Domain local* option and click OK. The new group object appears in the Rome OU.

Question 2	What must you do to enable the members of the Rome Backup group to perform backup operations on the local system?

5. Repeat steps 2 to 4 to create a domain local group called **Rome Printing**.

Question 3	What must you do to enable the members of the Rome Printing group to manage the queued print jobs on selected printers?

End of exercise. You can leave the windows open for the next exercise.

Exercise 15.3	Creating Global Groups
Overview	In this exercise, you create global groups using the Active Directory Administrative Center console.
Mindset	What is the function of the global groups in a group nesting arrangement?
Completion time	10 minutes

1. On the SVR-DC-A computer, in the *Active Directory Administrative Center* console, expand the adatum (local) node in the left pane and select the Rome OU you created in Exercise 15.1.

2. In the right pane, select New > Group. The Create Group dialog box appears (see Figure 15-4).

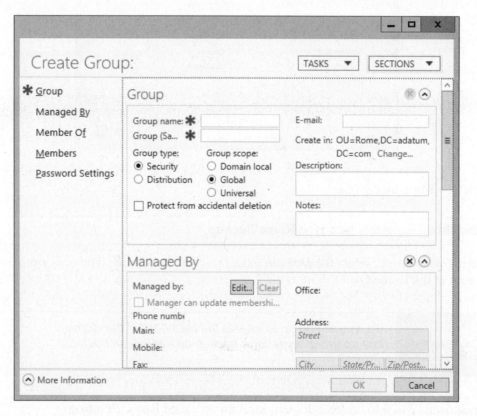

Figure 15-4
The Create Group dialog box

3. In the *Group name* text box, type **Backup Managers**.

4. Under *Group scope*, select Global and click OK. The new group appears in the Rome OU.

5. Repeat steps 2 to 4 to create a global group called **Print Managers** in the Rome OU.

6. Repeat steps 2 to 4 to create a global group called **Rome Managers** in the Rome OU.

End of exercise. You can leave the windows open for the next exercise.

Lab Challenge	Nesting Groups
Overview	By nesting groups in AD DS, you can create a system per privileges that allows any number of personnel changes.
Completion time	15 minutes

To complete this challenge, you must nest the groups you created previously in this lab so that the members of the Print Managers group will receive the privileges assigned to the Rome Printing group, and the Backup Managers group will receive the privileges assigned to the Rome Backup group.

List the changes you must make to complete the challenge.

End of exercise. You can leave the windows open for the next exercise.

Exercise 15.4	Delegating Administration
Overview	In this exercise, you use the Delegation of Control Wizard to grant Active Directory permissions to specific groups.
Mindset	How do you delegate administrative privileges to users without giving them full control?
Completion time	10 minutes

1. On the SVR-DC-A computer, in the *Active Directory Users and Computers* console, right-click the Rome OU and, from the context menu, select Delegate Control. The Delegation of Control Wizard appears, displaying the Welcome page.

2. Click Next. The Users or Groups page appears.

3. Click Add, The Select Users, Computers, or Groups dialog box appears.

4. In the *Enter the object names to select* box, type **Rome Managers** and click OK. The group appears on the Users or Groups list.

5. Click Next. The Tasks to Delegate page appears (see Figure 15-5).

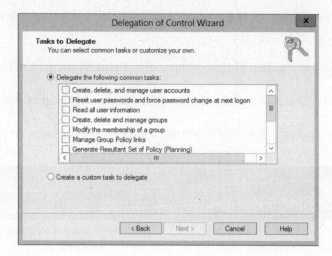

Figure 15-5
The Tasks to Delegate page in the Delegation of Control Wizard

6. In the *Delegate the following common tasks* list, select the following check boxes:

- Create, delete, and manage user accounts

- Create, delete, and manage groups

- Modify the membership of a group

7. Click Next. The *Completing the Delegation of Control Wizard* page appears.

8. Click Finish.

End of lab.

LAB 16
CREATING GROUP POLICY OBJECTS

BEFORE YOU BEGIN

The lab environment consists of three servers connected to a local area network, one of which is configured to function as the domain controller for a domain called *adatum.com*. The computers required for this lab are listed in Table 16-1.

Table 16-1
Computers Required for Lab 16

Computer	Operating System	Computer Name
Domain controller 1	Windows Server 2012	SVR-DC-A
Member server 2	Windows Server 2012	SVR-MBR-B
Member server 3	Windows Server 2012	SVR-MBR-C

In addition to the computers, you also require the software listed in Table 16-2 to complete Lab 16.

Table 16-2
Software Required for Lab 16

Software	Location
Lab 16 student worksheet	Lab16_worksheet.docx (provided by instructor)

Working with Lab Worksheets

Each lab in this manual requires that you answer questions, take screen shots, and perform other activities that you will document in a worksheet named for the lab, such as Lab16_worksheet.docx. It is recommended that you use a USB flash drive to store your worksheets, so you can submit them to your instructor for review. As you perform the exercises in each lab, open the appropriate worksheet file, fill in the required information, and save the file to your flash drive.

After completing this lab, you will be able to:

- Create a starter GPO

- Create new GPOs

- Link GPOs to organizational units

- Confirm GPO application to OU

Estimated lab time: 55 minutes

Exercise 16.1	Installing Group Policy Management
Overview	In this exercise, you install the Group Policy Management tools that enable you to create and manage GPOs from a member server.
Mindset	What is the most convenient location to manage your enterprise Group Policy strategy?
Completion time	10 minutes

1. Log on to the SVR-MBR-B computer, using the domain Administrator account and the password **Pa$$w0rd**. In Server Manager, click Manage > Add Roles and Features. The Add Roles and Features Wizard appears, displaying the *Before you begin* page.

2. Click Next. The *Select installation type* page appears.

3. Click Next. The *Select destination server* page appears.

4. Click Next. The *Select server roles* page appears.

5. Click Next. The *Select features* page appears.

6. Scroll down and select the Group Policy Management check box.

7. Click Next. The *Confirm installation selections* page appears.

8. Click Install. The *Installation progress* page appears as the wizard installs the selected features.

9. Click Close. The wizard closes.

10. Click Tools. The Tools menu appears, which now contains the Group Policy Management console.

11. Press Alt+Prt Scr to take a screen shot of the Tools menu. Press Ctrl+V to paste the image on the page provided in the Lab 16 worksheet file.

End of exercise. Leave all windows open for the next exercise.

Exercise 16.2	Creating a Starter GPO
Overview	In this exercise, you create a new starter GPO containing settings that you want all your new GPOs to receive.
Mindset	How do I avoid configuring the same settings in many GPOs?
Completion time	10 minutes

1. On SVR-MBR-B, in Server Manager, click Tools > Group Policy Management. The Group Policy Management console appears.

2. In the left pane, expand the Forest: adatum.com node, the Domains node, and the adatum.com node (see Figure 16-1).

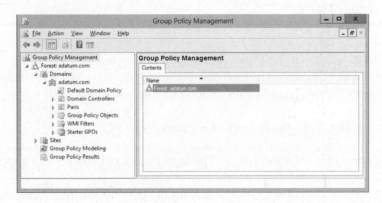

Figure 16-1
The Group Policy Management console

3. Right-click the Starter GPOs node and, from the context menu, click New. The New Starter GPO dialog box appears.

4. In the Name text box, type **Branch Office** and click OK. The new starter GPO appears in the console.

5. Expand the Starter GPOs node, right-click the Branch Office GPO, and, from the context menu, select Edit. The Group Policy Starter GPO Editor console appears.

6. In the left pane, browse to the Computer Configuration > Administrative Templates > Network > Offline Files folder.

7. In the right pane, double-click the *Prohibit user configuration of offline files* policy. The *Prohibit user configuration of offline files* dialog box appears.

8. Select the Enabled option and click OK.

9. Open the *Remove "Make Available Offline" Command* dialog box and enable it as you did before, clicking OK when finished.

10. Press Alt+Prt Scr to take a screen shot of the Group Policy Starter GPO Editor console, showing the two policies you configured. Press Ctrl+V to paste the image on the page provided in the Lab 16 worksheet file.

11. Close the Group Policy Starter GPO Editor console.

End of exercise. Leave all windows open for the next exercise.

Exercise 16.3	Creating Group Policy Objects
Overview	To complete this exercise, you use the starter GPO you created previously to create a new GPO with additional settings.
Mindset	How do I use a starter GPO to create additional GPOs?
Completion time	10 minutes

1. On SVR-MBR-B, in the Group Policy Management console, right-click the Branch Office Starter GPO you created in Exercise 16.2, and, from the context menu, select New GPO from Starter GPO. The New GPO dialog box appears.

2. In the Name text box, type **Paris Lockdown** and click OK.

3. Expand the Group Policy Objects node. The new Paris Lockdown GPO appears.

4. Right-click the Paris Lockdown GPO and, from the context menu, select Edit. The Group Policy Management Editor console appears (see Figure 16-2).

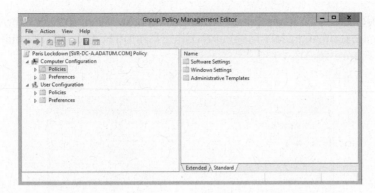

Figure 16-2
The Group Policy Management Editor console

5. Now, browse to the Computer Configuration > Policies > Windows Settings > Security Settings > Account Policies > Account Lockout Policy folder.

6. Open the following three policies, click the Define this policy setting check box, and configure them with the specified values:

   - *Account lockout duration* – 30 minutes

   - *Account lockout threshold* – 5 invalid Logon attempts

   - *Reset account lockout after* – 30 minutes

7. Press Alt+Prt Scr to take a screen shot of the *Reset account lockout after Properties* sheet, showing the changes you made to its configuration. Press Ctrl+V to paste the image on the page provided in the Lab 16 worksheet file.

8. Close the Group Policy Management Editor console.

End of exercise. Leave all windows open for the next exercise.

Exercise 16.4	Linking a Group Policy Object
Overview	To complete this exercise, you must apply the GPO you have made to an organizational unit, and control its application using security filtering.
Mindset	How do you control which computers receive the settings in a specific GPO?
Completion time	10 minutes

1. On SVR-MBR-B, in the Group Policy Management console, right-click the Paris OU and, in the context menu, select Link an Existing GPO. The Select GPO dialog box appears (see Figure 16-3).

Figure 16-3
The Select GPO dialog box

2. In the Group Policy Objects list, select Paris Lockdown and click OK. The GPO appears in the right pane, on the Linked Group Policy Objects tab of Paris OU.

3. Click the Group Policy Inheritance tab. The list of GPOs now contains the Paris Lockdown and the Default Doman Policy GPO.

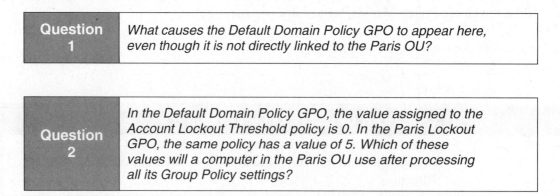

Question 1	*What causes the Default Domain Policy GPO to appear here, even though it is not directly linked to the Paris OU?*

Question 2	*In the Default Domain Policy GPO, the value assigned to the Account Lockout Threshold policy is 0. In the Paris Lockout GPO, the same policy has a value of 5. Which of these values will a computer in the Paris OU use after processing all its Group Policy settings?*

4. In the Group Policy Objects node, select the Paris Lockdown GPO (click OK if a message appears) and, in the right pane, look at the Scope tab.

5. In the Security Filtering area, click Add. The Select User, Computer, or Group dialog box appears.

6. In the *Enter the object name to select* text box, type **Servers** and click OK. The Servers group appears in the Security Filtering list.

7. Select the Authenticated Users group and click Remove.

8. Click OK to confirm the removal.

9. Press Alt+Prt Scr to take a screen shot of the Group Policy Management console, showing the changes you made to the Security Filtering configuration. Press Ctrl+V to paste the image on the page provided in the Lab 16 worksheet file.

End of exercise. Leave all windows open for the next exercise.

Lab Challenge	Confirming GPO Application
Overview	To complete this challenge, you must demonstrate that the Group Policy settings you have created in the Paris Lockdown GPO have taken effect on SVR-MBR-C.
Mindset	How can you tell when Group Policy settings are active?
Completion time	15 minutes

The SVR-MBR-C computer is located in the Paris OU, and is a member of the Server group. It should, therefore, receive the settings you configured in the Paris Lockdown GPO. Prove that this is the case by taking screen shots of the computer that demonstrate that the Account Lockout Threshold value has changed.

NOTE	*Before you begin working on SVR-MBR-C, open an administrative command prompt and run the **gpupdate/force** command to refresh the computer's Group Policy settings.*

End of lab.

LAB 17
CONFIGURING SECURITY POLICIES

THIS LAB CONTAINS THE FOLLOWING EXERCISES AND ACTIVITIES: _ _ _ _

Exercise 17.1   Configuring Security Policies

Lab Challenge   Assigning User Rights

Exercise 17.2   Configuring Audit Policies

Lab Challenge   Viewing Auditing Data

BEFORE YOU BEGIN

The lab environment consists of three servers connected to a local area network, one of which is configured to function as the domain controller for a domain called *adatum.com*. The computers required for this lab are listed in Table 17-1.

Table 17-1
Computers Required for Lab 17

Computer	Operating System	Computer Name
Domain controller 1	Windows Server 2012	SVR-DC-A
Member server 2	Windows Server 2012	SVR-MBR-B
Member server 3	Windows Server 2012	SVR-MBR-C

In addition to the computers, you also require the software listed in Table 17-2 to complete Lab 17.

Table 17-2
Software Required for Lab 17

Software required for Lab 17Software	Location
Lab 17 student worksheet	Lab17_worksheet.docx (provided by instructor)

Working with Lab Worksheets

Each lab in this manual requires that you answer questions, take screen shots, and perform other activities that you will document in a worksheet named for the lab, such as Lab17_worksheet.docx. It is recommended that you use a USB flash drive to store your worksheets, so you can submit them to your instructor for review. As you perform the exercises in each lab, open the appropriate worksheet file, fill in the required information, and save the file to your flash drive.

After completing this lab, you will be able to:

- Configure security policies

- Configure and assign user rights

- Configure audit policies

Estimated lab time: 60 minutes

Exercise 17.1	Configuring Security Policies
Overview	In this exercise, you examine the default Security Policy settings for your domain and then create a GPO containing new and revised settings.
Mindset	How can you control access to your network computers using security policies?
Completion time	15 minutes

1. Log on to the SVR-MBR-B computer, using the domain Administrator account and the password **Pa$$w0rd**. Install the Group Policy Management feature using the Add Roles and Features Wizard, just as you did in Exercise 16.1.

2. In Server Manager, click Tools > Group Policy Management. The Group Policy Management console appears.

3. Browse to the Group Policy Objects folder.

Question 1	*How can you tell which of the policies in the Security Options folder have changed settings in the Default Domain Policy GPO?*

4. Press Alt+Prt Scr to take a screen shot showing the existing Security Options settings in the Default Domain Policy GPO. Press Ctrl+V to paste the image on the page provided in the Lab 17 worksheet file.

5. Right-click the Group Policy Objects folder and, on the context menu, click New. The New GPO dialog box appears.

6. In the Name text box, type **Revised Domain** and click OK. A new Revised Domain GPO appears in the Group Policy Objects folder.

7. Right-click the Revised Domain GPO and, in the context menu, click Edit. The Group Policy Management Editor console appears.

8. In the Group Policy Management Editor console, browse to the Computer Configuration > Policies > Windows Settings > Security Settings > Local Policies > Security Options folder.

9. In the Security Options folder, double-click the *Devices: Allowed to format and eject removable media policy*. The *Devices: Allowed to format and eject removable media policy* dialog box appears (see Figure 17-1).

Figure 17-1
The *Devices: Allowed to format and eject removable media policy* dialog box

10. Select the *Define this policy setting* check box, and in the drop-down list, select *Administrators and Interactive Users*. Then click OK.

11. Define and enable the following Security Options policies:

- Devices: Restrict CD-ROM access to locally logged on user only policy

- Devices: Restrict floppy access to locally logged on user only policy

- Network Security: Force logoff when logon hours expire

12. Close the Group Policy Management Editor console.

13. In the Group Policy Management console, right-click the adatum.com domain and, in the context menu, click Link an Existing GPO. The Select GPO dialog box appears.

14. Select the Revised Domain GPO and click OK.

15. Select the adatum.com domain and click the Linked Group Policy Objects tab in the right pane.

16. Select the Revised Domain GPO and click the *Move link up* arrow. The Revised Domain GPO now appears first in the list of linked GPOs.

Question 2	*Why is it necessary for the Revised Options GPO to appear first in the list?*

End of exercise. Leave all windows open for the next exercise.

Lab Challenge	Assigning User Rights
Overview	In this exercise, you add a selection of user rights assignments to the ones that already exist.
Completion time	15 minutes

Your organization has created a new job role called the director, and your job is to provide the new directors with the domain controller user rights they need to perform their jobs. The Directors group has already been created in the adatum.com domain. To complete this challenge, you must grant the Directors group the following user rights to all the domain controllers on the network, without interfering with any of the existing rights.

- Deny logon locally

- Add workstations to domain

- Force shutdown from a remote system

- Enable computer and user accounts to be trusted for delegation

- Manage auditing and security log

- Shut down the system

Write out the basic steps you have to perform to accomplish the challenge and then take a screen shot showing the user rights you configured and press Ctrl+V to paste the image on the page provided in the Lab 17 worksheet file.

End of exercise. Leave all windows open for the next exercise.

Exercise 17.2	Configuring Audit Policies
Overview	In this exercise, you configure the auditing policies to monitor account logons and access to specific objects.
Mindset	How can you use the auditing capabilities in Windows Server 2012 to increase the security of your network without overwhelming yourself with data?
Completion time	20 minutes

1. On SVR-MBR-B, in the Group Policy Management console, create a new GPO called **Audit Policies** and open it in the Group Policy Management Editor.

2. Browse to the Computer Configuration > Policies > Windows Settings > Security Settings > Local Policies > Audit Policy node. The audit policies appear in the right pane.

3. Double-click the *Audit account logon events* policy. The *Audit account logon events Properties* sheet appears.

4. Select the *Define these policy settings* check box.

5. Select the Failure check box, clear the Success check box, and click OK.

Question 3	Why, in this case, is the auditing of event failures more useful than the auditing of successes?

6. Double-click the Audit object access policy. The Audit object access Properties sheet appears.

7. Select the Define these policy settings check box.

8. Select the Failure and the Success check boxes and click OK.

9. Press Alt+Prt Scr to take a screen shot showing the policies you configured. Press Ctrl+V to paste the image on the page provided in the Lab 17 worksheet file.

10. Under Security Settings, select the Event Log node.

11. In the right pane, double-click the Maximum security log size policy.

12. Select the *Define this policy setting* check box, leave the spinbox value at 16384 kilobytes, and click OK.

Question 4	Why is it prudent to limit the event log size when using auditing.

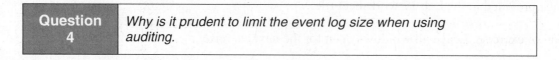

13. Close the Group Policy Management Editor console.

14. Link the Audit Policies GPO to the adatum.com domain.

15. Click the File Explorer icon on the Taskbar. The File Explorer window appears.

16. In the left pane, browse to the C: drive on the local computer.

17. Right-click the C:\Windows folder and, in the context menu, click Properties. The Windows Properties sheet appears.

18. Click the Security tab.

19. Click Advanced. The Advanced Security Settings for Windows dialog box appears.

20. Click the Auditing tab (see Figure 17-2).

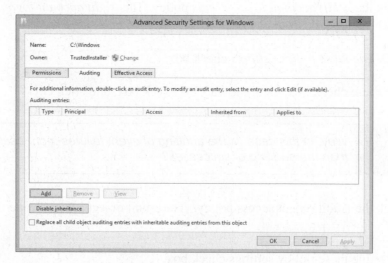

Figure 17-2
The Advanced Security Settings for Windows dialog box

21. Click Add. The Auditing Entry for Windows dialog box appears.

22. Click Select a Principal. The Select User, Computer, Service Account, or Group dialog box appears.

23. In the *Enter the object name to select* text box, type **Administrator** and click OK.

24. Select the Full Control check box and click OK.

25. Click OK to close the Advanced Security Settings for Windows dialog box.

26. Click Continue to bypass error messages, if necessary. Click OK to close the Windows Properties sheet.

27. Open an administrative Command Prompt window and type **gpupdate /force** to update the system's Group Policy settings.

End of exercise. Leave all windows open for the next exercise.

Lab Challenge	Viewing Auditing Data
Overview	To complete this exercise, you must demonstrate that your SVR-MBR-B computer is actually gathering the auditing data you configured its policies to gather.
Mindset	How do you display auditing data?
Completion time	10 minutes

To complete this challenge, display the auditing data you configured your server to gather in Exercise 17.2. Press Alt+Prt Scr to take a screen shot showing a sample of the data you gathered. Press Ctrl+V to paste the image on the page provided in the Lab 17 worksheet file.

End of lab.

LAB 18
CONFIGURING APPLICATION RESTRICTION POLICIES

THIS LAB CONTAINS THE FOLLOWING EXERCISES AND ACTIVITIES:

Exercise 18.1   Configuring Software Restriction Policies

Exercise 18.2   Using AppLocker

Lab Challenge   Creating Additional Rules

BEFORE YOU BEGIN

The lab environment consists of three servers connected to a local area network, one of which is configured to function as the domain controller for a domain called *adatum.com*. The computers required for this lab are listed in Table 18-1.

Table 18-1
Computers Required for Lab 18

Computer	Operating System	Computer Name
Domain controller 1	Windows Server 2012	SVR-DC-A
Member server 2	Windows Server 2012	SVR-MBR-B
Member server 3	Windows Server 2012	SVR-MBR-C

In addition to the computers, you also require the software listed in Table 18-2 to complete Lab 18.

Table 18-2
Software Required for Lab 18

Software	Location
Lab 18 student worksheet	Lab18_worksheet.docx (provided by instructor)

Working with Lab Worksheets

Each lab in this manual requires that you answer questions, take screen shots, and perform other activities that you will document in a worksheet named for the lab, such as Lab18_worksheet.docx. It is recommended that you use a USB flash drive to store your worksheets, so you can submit them to your instructor for review. As you perform the exercises in each lab, open the appropriate worksheet file, fill in the required information, and save the file to your flash drive.

After completing this lab, you will be able to:

■ Create software restriction policies

■ Configure AppLocker

Estimated lab time: 40 minutes

Exercise 18.1	Creating Software Restriction Policies
Overview	In this exercise, you create a rule that prevents users from running a specific program.
Mindset	How can you stop network users from wasting time with games and other non-productive programs?
Completion time	20 minutes

1. Log on to the SVR-MBR-B computer, using the domain Administrator account and the password **Pa$$w0rd**. Open Server Manager, then click Tools > Group Policy Management. The Group Policy Management console appears.

2. Browse to the Group Policy Objects folder.

3. Right-click the Group Policy Objects folder and, on the context menu, click New. The New GPO dialog box appears.

4. In the Name text box, type **Software Restrictions** and click OK. A new Software Restrictions GPO appears in the Group Policy Objects folder.

5. Right-click the Software Restrictions GPO and, in the context menu, click Edit. The Group Policy Management Editor console appears.

6. In the Group Policy Management Editor console, browse to the Computer Configuration > Policies > Windows Settings > Security Settings > Software Restriction Policies folder.

7. Right-click the Software Restriction Policies folder and, in the context menu, click New Software Restriction Policies. The default policies and subfolders appear.

8. Right-click the Additional Rules folder and, in the contents menu, select New Hash Rule. The New Hash Rule dialog box appears (see Figure 18-1).

Figure 18-1
The New Hash Rule dialog box

9. Click Browse. An Open combo box appears.

10. Browse to and select the C:\Windows\regedit file. Click Open. The information to be hashed appears in the File Information box.

11. Click OK. The hash rule appears in the Additional Rules folder.

Question 1	*What problem would occur if you changed the default software restriction to Disallowed and configured a hash rule setting the regedit.exe file to Unrestricted?*

12. Close the Group Policy Management Editor console.

13. In the Group Policy Management console, right-click the adatum.com domain and, in the context menu, click Link an Existing GPO. The Select GPO dialog box appears.

14. Select the Software Restrictions GPO and click OK.

15. On SVR-MBR-C, restart the computer.

16. When the computer restarts, press CTRL+ALT+DEL and log on using the **Adatum\Administrator** account with the password **Pa$$w0rd**.

17. Click the File Explorer button on the Taskbar. The File Explorer window appears.

18. Browse to the C:\Windows folder on the local system and double-click the regedit file. A message box appears, informing you that access to the file is blocked.

19. Press Alt+Prt Scr to take a screen shot showing the message box. Press Ctrl+V to paste the image on the page provided in the Lab 18 worksheet file.

20. On SVR-MBR-B, in the Group Policy Management console, click the Linked Group Policy Objects tab.

21. Right-click the Software Restriction GPO link on adatum.com, and click to clear the Link Enabled checkmark. A message box appears, prompting you to confirm your action.

22. Click OK.

End of exercise. Leave all windows open for the next exercise.

Exercise 18.2	Using AppLocker
Overview	In this exercise, you create rules governing program access using AppLocker.
Mindset	How does the process of creating AppLocker rules differ from that of creating software restriction policies?
Completion time	20 minutes

1. On the SVR-MBR-B computer, in Server Manager, click Tools > Group Policy Management. The Group Policy Management console appears.

2. Browse to the Group Policy Objects folder.

3. Right-click the Group Policy Objects folder and, on the context menu, click New. The New GPO dialog box appears.

4. In the Name text box, type **AppLocker Rules** and click OK. A new AppLocker Rules GPO appears in the Group Policy Objects folder.

5. Right-click the AppLocker Rules GPO and, in the context menu, click Edit. The Group Policy Management Editor console appears.

6. In the Group Policy Management Editor console, browse to the Computer Configuration > Policies > Windows Settings > Security Settings > Application Control Policies > AppLocker folder.

7. Expand the AppLocker folder (see Figure 18-2).

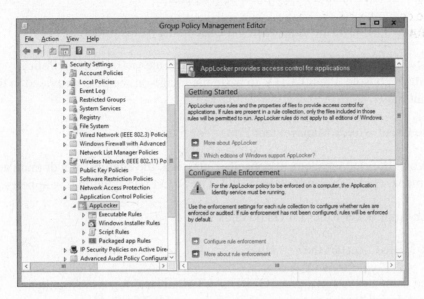

Figure 18-2
The AppLocker folder

8. Select the Executable Rules folder.

9. Right-click the Executable Rules folder and, on the context menu, click Automatically Generate Rules. The Automatically Generate Executable Rules Wizard appears, displaying the *Folder and Permissions* page.

10. Click Next. The *Rule Preferences* page appears.

11. Click Next. The *Review Rules* page appears.

12. Click Create. A message box appears, asking if you want to create default rules.

13. Click Yes. The rules appear in the Executable Rules folder.

14. Repeat steps 9 to 13 twice to create the default rules in the Windows Installer Rules and Script Rules folders.

15. Right-click the Executable Rules folder and, on the context menu, click Create New Rule. The Create Executable Rules Wizard appears, displaying the *Before you begin* page.

16. Click Next. The *Permissions* page appears.

17. Select the Deny option and click Next. The *Conditions* page appears.

18. Select the File hash option and click Next. The *File Hash* page appears.

19. Click Browse files. An Open combo box appears.

20. Browse to the *regedit* file and click Open.

21. Click Next. The *Name and Description* page appears.

22. Click Create. The new rule appears in the Executable Rules folder.

23. Press Alt+Prt Scr to take a screen shot showing the rules in the Group Policy Management console. Press Ctrl+V to paste the image on the page provided in the Lab 18 worksheet file.

24. Close the Group Policy Management Editor console.

25. In the Group Policy Management console, right-click the adatum.com domain and, in the context menu, click Link an Existing GPO. The Select GPO dialog box appears.

26. Select the AppLocker Rules GPO and click OK.

27. On SVR-MBR-C, restart the computer.

28. When the computer restarts, press CTRL+ALT+DEL and log on using the **Adatum\Administrator** account with the password **Pa$$w0rd**.

29. Click the File Explorer button on the Taskbar. The File Explorer window appears.

30. Browse to the C:\Windows folder on the local system and double-click the regedit file. The Registry Editor program loads.

31. Close the Registry Editor.

32. In Server Manager, click Tools > Services. The Services console appears.

33. Right-click the Application Identity service and, in the context menu, click Start. The service starts.

34. In File Explorer, browse to the C:\Windows folder on the local system and double-click the regedit file.

35. A message box appears, informing you that access to the file is blocked.

Question 2	Why is it necessary to start the Application Identity service before the AppLocker rules take effect?

End of exercise. Close any open windows before you begin the next exercise.

Lab Challenge	Creating Additional Rules
Overview	To complete this challenge, you must create a new GPO containing additional AppLocker rules.
Completion time	20 minutes

On the SVR-MBR-B computer, create a new GPO called *AppLocker 2* and create a rule that allows members of the Administrators group to run all digitally signed files published by Microsoft.

Press Alt+Prt Scr to take a screen shot of the Group Policy Management Editor console showing the rule you created and press Ctrl+V to paste the image on the page provided in the Lab 18 worksheet file.

End of lab.

LAB 19
CONFIGURING WINDOWS FIREWALL

THIS LAB CONTAINS THE FOLLOWING EXERCISES AND ACTIVITIES:

Exercise 19.1   Installing Internet Information Services

Exercise 19.2   Testing IIS Connectivity

Exercise 19.3   Allowing Apps through the Windows Firewall Control Panel

Exercise 19.4   Creating Windows Firewall Rules

Lab Challenge   Creating an FTP Server Rule

BEFORE YOU BEGIN

The lab environment consists of three servers connected to a local area network, which are part of a domain called *adatum.com*. The computers required for this lab are listed in Table 19-1.

Table 19-1
Computers Required for Lab 19

Computer	Operating System	Computer Name
Domain controller 1	Windows Server 2012	SVR-DC-A
Member server 2	Windows Server 2012	SVR-MBR-B
Member server 3	Windows Server 2012	SVR-MBR-C

In addition to the computers, you also require the software listed in Table 19-2 to complete Lab 19.

Table 19-2
Software Required for Lab 19

Software	Location
Lab 19 student worksheet	Lab19_worksheet.docx (provided by instructor)

Working with Lab Worksheets

Each lab in this manual requires that you answer questions, take screen shots, and perform other activities that you will document in a worksheet named for the lab, such as Lab19_worksheet.docx. It is recommended that you use a USB flash drive to store your worksheets, so you can submit them to your instructor for review. As you perform the exercises in each lab, open the appropriate worksheet file, fill in the required information, and save the file to your flash drive.

After completing this lab, you will be able to:

■ Install and check connectivity of IIS websites

■ Allow apps through Windows Firewall control panel

■ Create Windows Firewall Rules

Estimated lab time: 60 minutes

Exercise 19.1	Installing Internet Information Services
Overview	In this exercise, you install IIS to configure SVR-MBR-B as a web server, which you will use later to demonstrate the functions of Windows Firewall.
Mindset	How can you use a firewall to limit access to a web server?
Completion time	15 minutes

1. Log on to the SVR-MBR-B computer, using the domain Administrator account and the password **Pa$$w0rd**. Open Server Manager, then click Tools > Group Policy Management. The Group Policy Management console appears.

2. Click Next. The *Select Installation Type* page appears.

3. Leave the *Role-based or feature-based installation* radio button selected and click Next. The *Select Destination Server* page appears.

4. Click Next to accept the default local server. The *Select Server Roles* page appears.

5. Select the Web Server (IIS) check box. The *Add features that are required for Web Server (IIS)?* page appears.

6. Click *Add features*.

7. Click Next. The *Select features* page appears.

8. Click Next. The *Web Server Role (IIS)* page appears.

9. Click Next. The *Select Role Services* page appears.

10. Click Next. The *Confirm installation selections* page appears.

11. Click Install. The *Installation Progress* page appears as the wizard installs the selected roles and features.

12. Click Close after successful installation.

13. In Server Manager, click Tools > Internet Information Services (IIS) Manager. The Internet Information Services (IIS) Manager console appears (see Figure 19-1).

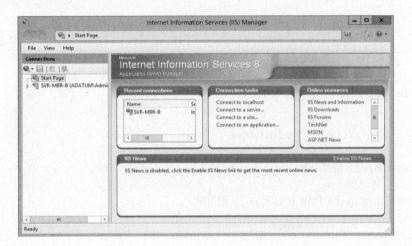

Figure 19-1
The Internet Information Services (IIS) Manager console

14. In the left pane, expand the SVR-MBR-B container. A message box appears, offering Microsoft Web Platform.

15. Click No.

16. Expand the Sites folder.

17. Right-click the Sites folder and, from the context menu, select Add Website. The Add Website dialog box appears (see Figure 19-2).

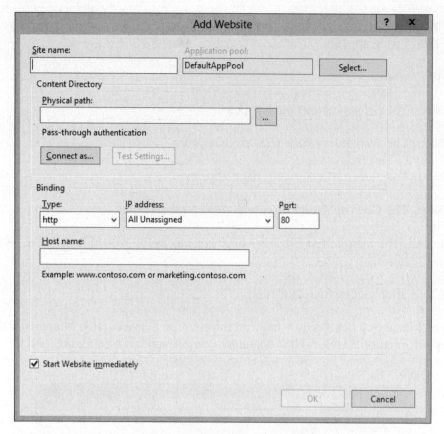

Figure 19-2
The Add Website dialog box

18. In the *Site name* text box, type **Intranet**.

19. In the *Physical path* text box, type **c:\inetpub\wwwroot**.

20. Change the value in the Port text box to **8888**.

21. Click OK. The new Intranet website appears in the Sites folder.

Question 1	What URLs can you use in your computer's browser to test the functionality of the intranet website you just created?

22. Take a screen shot of the Internet Information Services (IIS) Manager console, showing the new site you created, by pressing Alt+Prt Scr, and then paste the resulting image into the Lab 19 worksheet file in the page provided by pressing Ctrl+V.

23. Close the Internet Information Services (IIS) Manager console.

End of exercise. Leave all windows open for the next exercise.

Exercise 19.2	Testing IIS Connectivity
Overview	In this exercise, you test the default connectivity to the web server you just installed and configured.
Mindset	What is the default Windows Firewall configuration?
Completion time	15 minutes

1. On SVR-MBR-B, open the Start screen and click the Internet Explorer tile. An Internet Explorer window appears.

2. In the address box, type **http://127.0.0.1** and press Enter. The browser displays the splash screen that IIS8 installs as the home page of the default website, indicating that IIS is installed and running properly on the computer.

3. Next, test the intranet website by using the URL you specified in Exercise 19.1. The browser successfully connects to the website, indicating that it is configured correctly.

4. Log on to the SVR-MBR-C computer, using the domain Administrator account and the password **Pa$$w0rd**. Open Internet Explorer and attempt to access the IIS web server running on SVR-MBR-B by typing **http://svr-mbr-b** in the address box and pressing Enter. The browser connects to the web server.

5. Now, try to connect to the intranet website from SVR-MBR-C. The browser fails to connect to the intranet web server.

Question 2	*What possible reason would explain why you are unable to connect to the Intranet site on your computer's web server, using a browser on another computer.*

6. Back on SVR-MBR-B, in Server Manager, click the Local Server node and then click the Windows Firewall link. The Windows Firewall control panel appears, as shown in Figure 19-3.

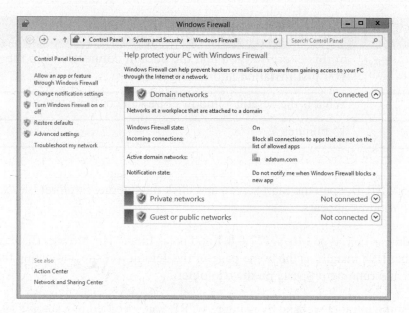

Figure 19-3
The Windows Firewall control panel

7. Click Turn Windows Firewall on or off. The Customize settings for each type of network window appears.

8. Under Domain network settings, select the Turn off Windows Firewall (not recommended) option.

9. Take a screen shot of the Customize settings for each type of network window, showing the setting you changed, by pressing Alt+Prt Scr, and then paste the resulting image into the Lab 19 worksheet file in the page provided by pressing Ctrl+V.

10. Click OK.

11. Return to the SVR-MBR-C computer and try again to access both of the sites on the web server using Internet Explorer. The browser now successfully connects to both websites on the server and displays the IIS8 splash screen.

12. Clear the Internet Explorer cache on SVR-MBR-C by clicking Tools > Internet Options. The Internet Options dialog box appears.

13. Under Browsing History, click the Delete button. The Delete Browsing History dialog box appears.

14. Click Delete. Then click OK to close the Internet Options dialog box.

Question 3	Why is it necessary to clear the cache before you retest the web server connections?

15. Back on SVR-MBR-B in the Windows Firewall control panel, open the *Customize settings for each type of network* window again, by clicking the *Turn Windows Firewall on or off* link.

16. Under *Domain network location settings*, select the *Turn on Windows Firewall* option and click OK.

Question 4	Why can you not simply leave Windows Firewall turned off when you deploy an actual web server?

End of exercise. Leave all windows open for the next exercise.

Exercise 19.3	Allowing Apps through the Windows Firewall Control Panel
Overview	Windows Firewall is preventing some clients from connecting to the web server.
Mindset	What access to Windows Firewall does the Control Panel provide?
Completion time	15 minutes

1. On your SVR-MBR-B computer, in the Windows Firewall control panel, click *Allow an app or feature through Windows Firewall*. The *Allow apps to communicate through Windows Firewall* window appears, as shown in Figure 19-4.

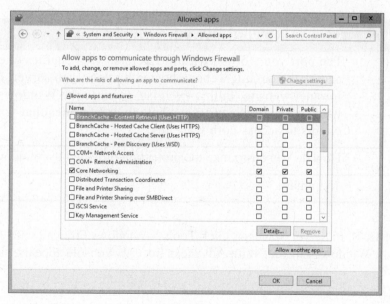

Figure 19-4
The *Allow apps to communicate through Windows Firewall* window

2. Scroll down in the *Allowed programs and features* list, and clear all the check boxes for the Secure World Wide Web Services (HTTPS) and World Wide Web Services (HTTP) entries.

3. Take a screen shot of the *Allow apps to communicate through Windows Firewall* window, showing the setting you changed, by pressing Alt+Prt Scr, and then paste the resulting image into the Lab 19 worksheet file in the page provided by pressing Ctrl+V.

4. Click OK.

5. On SVR-MBR-C, try again to connect to the default website at **http://svr-mbr-b**.

Question 5	Why are you now unable to connect to the website from the client?

6. On SCR-MBR-B, open the *Allow programs to communicate through Windows Firewall* window again and select the three Secure World Wide Web Services (HTTPS) check boxes and the three World Wide Web Services (HTTP) check boxes. Then, click OK.

7. Now, back at SVR-MBR-C, test the connection to the intranet website.

Question 6	Why are you unable to connect to the intranet site from the client?

End of exercise. Leave all windows open for the next exercise.

Exercise 19.4	Creating Windows Firewall Rules
Overview	The port you worked with in Exercise 19.3 enables clients to access the default website hosted by your web server, but not the intranet website. In this exercise, you use the Windows Firewall with Advanced Security console to create rules that will enable clients to access both websites.
Mindset	How do you customize the protection provided by Windows Firewall?
Completion time	15 minutes

1. On SVR-MBR-B, in Server Manager, click Tools > Windows Firewall with Advanced Security. The Windows Firewall With Advanced Security console appears, as shown in Figure 19-5.

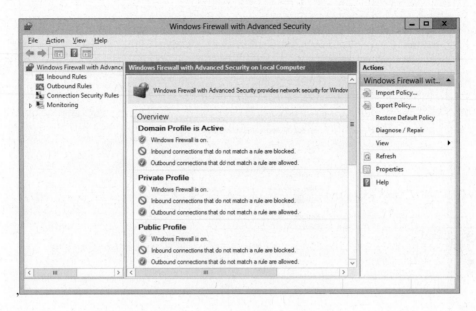

Figure 19-5
The Windows Firewall with Advanced Security console

2. Select the Inbound Rules container. The list of default inbound rules appears.

3. Scroll down to the bottom of the list and locate the rules for World Wide Web Services (HTTP Traffic-In).

4. Double-click the rule and examine its properties.

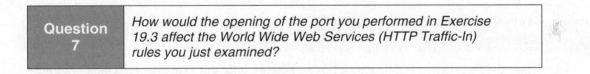

Question 7	How would the opening of the port you performed in Exercise 19.3 affect the World Wide Web Services (HTTP Traffic-In) rules you just examined?

5. Click OK to close the WWW Services (HTTP Traffic-In) Properties sheet.

6. Right-click the Inbound Rules container and, from the context menu, select New Rule. The New Inbound Rule Wizard launches, displaying the *Rule Type* page, as shown in Figure 19-6.

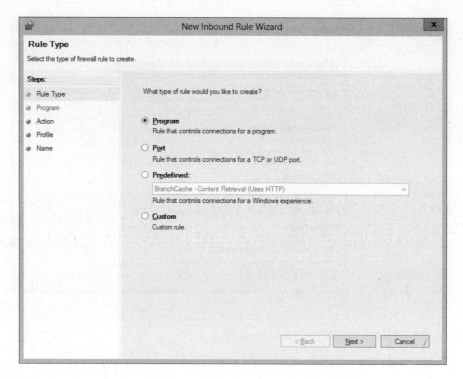

Figure 19-6
The New Inbound Rule Wizard

7. Select the Port option and click Next. The *Protocol and Ports* page appears.

8. Leave the default TCP and *Specific local ports* options selected. In the *Specific local ports* text box, type **80, 8888** and click Next. The *Action* page appears.

9. Leave the default *Allow the connection* option selected and click Next. The *Profile* page appears.

10. Clear the Private and Public check boxes, leaving only the Domain check box selected, and then click Next. The *Name* page appears.

11. In the Name text box, type **Lab Web Server – Ports 80 & 8888** and click Finish. The wizard creates and enables the new rule and then adds it to the Inbound Rules list.

Question 8	*How would the rule creation procedure you just performed differ if you wanted to restrict client access to the intranet site to computers on the local network only?*

12. Double-click the rule you just created. The Lab Web Server – Ports 80 & 8888 Properties sheet appears.

13. Take a screen shot of the Properties sheet for the new rule by pressing Alt+Prt Scr, and then paste the resulting image into the Lab 19 worksheet file in the page provided by pressing Ctrl+V.

14. Close OK to close the Properties sheet. On SVR-MBR-C, repeat your attempts to connect to both web servers.

Question 9	*What are the results, and why are they different from the results you experienced with the program exception?*

End of exercise. Close any open windows before you begin the next exercise.

Lab Challenge	Creating an FTP Server Rule
Overview	To complete this challenge, you must configure Windows Firewall to allow incoming traffic to reach an FTP server running on the computer.
Completion time	15 minutes

On SVR-MBR-B, using Windows Firewall with Advanced Security, create rules that will permit all possible traffic generated by FTP clients to reach an FTP server running on SCR-MBR-B.

Take a screen shot of the New Inbound Rule Wizard page showing the operative properties of the rule by pressing Alt+Prt Scr, and then paste the resulting image into the Lab 19 worksheet file in the page provided by pressing Ctrl+V.

End of lab.

APPENDIX:
LAB SETUP GUIDE

INTRODUCTION

Instructors can use the MOAC lab manual for 70-410: Installing and Configuring Windows Server 2012 in any one of the following classroom learning environments:

- **Microsoft Labs Online (MLO).** Each student requires a basic workstation that accesses virtual machines hosted by servers on the Internet.
- **Classroom-based virtual machines.** Each student requires a server or workstation capable of running as many as three Windows Server 2012 virtual machines simultaneously, using a hypervisor product, such as Microsoft Hyper-V or Microsoft Virtual Server.
- **Individual classroom computers.** Each student (or group of students) requires three servers running Windows Server 2012, connected to an independent local area network.

Classrooms using the MLO option require no setup or preparation beyond the acquisition of credentials providing access to the MLO web site. Each MLO lab consists of an independent environment consisting of two or three virtual machines, with all required software already installed and configured. Students only have to log on and select the lab they want to complete.

For courses using a classroom-based virtual machine solution, each student must have a computer with sufficient memory and other hardware resources to support three instances of Windows Server 2012, each running in a separate virtual machine. The instructor or lab manager is responsible for outfitting the computers, and for selecting and installing the hypervisor product that will support the virtual machines.

For courses using traditional server hardware, without virtual machines, students must have three servers to complete all of the exercises in the lab manual. Each group of three servers must be connected to a separate local area network, or to a classroom network configured in such a way as to keep each student's traffic separate from the others. Here again, the instructor or lab manager is responsible for designing and implementing the hardware configuration for the classroom.

This document provides operating system setup instructions for each of the labs in the manual. For classroom-based solutions, either virtual or traditional, instructors or lab managers are responsible for deploying the operating systems needed for each lab and configuring them using the individual requirements for each lab, as described in the following sections.

This document includes step-by-step instructions for manual operating system installation and configuration. However, many schools already have procedures in place for automating the OS deployment and configuration processes. Any method is acceptable, as long as it provides the operating environment each lab requires.

LAB REQUIREMENTS

For each of the lab sections that follow, there is a table listing the configuration requirements for each of the two or three computers required to complete the lab exercises. The column headings in each table provide the computer names by which the servers are identified in the lab manual.

The MOAC lab system naming conventions are as follows:

- System type – Server (SVR) or workstation (WKSTN)
- Network role – Domain controller (DC), member server (MBR), or standalone (SO) server
- Instance – A single letter (A, B, or C) uniquely identifying the system in the lab

Thus, for example, a computer with the name SVR-DC-A is the first server configured as a domain controller in a particular lab.

Lab 1. Installing Servers

Because it requires students to install and upgrade servers, Lab 1 has some unique setup requirements. One server must be in a bare metal configuration, that is, with all the hardware necessary to install and run Windows Server 2012, but with its hard disk completely blank.

Lab 1 is unique in that it requires Windows Server 2008 R2 to be installed on two of its servers. One of these will be upgraded to Windows Server 2012 during the lab, and the other will function as the source system for a side-to-side migration.

Table 1
Lab 1 Configuration Requirements

SVR-SO-A	*SVR-SO-B*	*SVR-SO-C*
Bare metal server	Install Windows Server 2008 R2	Install Windows Server 2008 R2
Insert Windows Server 2012 installation disk	Set Time Zone	Set Time Zone
	Change Computer Name	Change Computer Name
	Install Web Server (IIS)	
	Install File Services with File Server Resource Manager	

Lab 2. Configuring Servers

Lab 2 introduces students to the setup procedures you must perform immediately after installing Windows Server 2012. For that purpose, you must first install a domain controller for a new domain. The students will then join a second, newly installed server to the domain during the lab.

Table 2
Lab 2 Configuration Requirements

SVR-DC-A	SVR-MBR-B
Install Windows Server 2012	Install Windows Server 2012
Set Time Zone	
Configure TCP/IP: IPv4 address: 10.0.0.1 Subnet Mask: 255.255.255.0 DNS Server 10.0.0.1	
Change Computer Name	
Install the Active Directory Domain Services role	
Promote the server to a domain controller for adatum.com	

Lab 3. Configuring Local Storage

This lab requires students to work with the Windows Server 2012 storage subsystem. To accommodate this, one of the three servers (SVR-MBR-C) must have three hard disks, in addition to the one on which the operating system is installed. This is, obviously, most easily accomplished in a virtual machine environment. The three disks can be any size, and should be in their newly installed—that is, offline—state at the beginning of the lab.

Table 3
Lab 3 Configuration Requirements

SVR-DC-A	SVR-MBR-B	SVR-MBR-C
Install Windows Server 2012	Install Windows Server 2012	Install Windows Server 2012
Set Time Zone	Set Time Zone	Set Time Zone
Configure TCP/IP: IPv4 address: 10.0.0.1 Subnet Mask: 255.255.255.0 DNS Server 10.0.0.1	Configure TCP/IP: IPv4 address: 10.0.0.2 Subnet Mask: 255.255.255.0 DNS Server 10.0.0.1	Configure TCP/IP: IPv4 address: 10.0.0.3 Subnet Mask: 255.255.255.0 DNS Server 10.0.0.1
Change Computer Name	Change Computer Name	Change Computer Name
Install the Active Directory Domain Services role	Join to adatum.com domain	Join to adatum.com domain
Promote the server to a domain controller for adatum.com		

Lab 4. Configuring File and Share Access

Lab 4 uses an additional hard disk to create and configure shares. The lab is designed to use the same hardware configuration as Lab 3, with three additional disks on SVR-MBR-C. However, it is also possible to complete the exercises with a single additional disk, or by using only the system disk. In these cases, the only changes needed will be to the drive letter that the students use to create the directories they will share.

Table 4
Lab 4 Configuration Requirements

SVR-DC-A	SVR-MBR-B	SVR-MBR-C
Install Windows Server 2012	Install Windows Server 2012	Install Windows Server 2012
Set Time Zone	Set Time Zone	Set Time Zone
Configure TCP/IP: IPv4 address: 10.0.0.1 Subnet Mask: 255.255.255.0 DNS Server 10.0.0.1	Configure TCP/IP: IPv4 address: 10.0.0.2 Subnet Mask: 255.255.255.0 DNS Server 10.0.0.1	Configure TCP/IP: IPv4 address: 10.0.0.3 Subnet Mask: 255.255.255.0 DNS Server 10.0.0.1
Change Computer Name	Change Computer Name	Change Computer Name
Install the Active Directory Domain Services role	Join to adatum.com domain	Join to adatum.com domain
Promote the server to a domain controller for adatum.com	Enable file sharing	Enable file sharing
Create a domain user account with the name Student		Initialize the three additional hard disks
		Create a simple volume on each of the three additional disks

Lab 5. Configuring Print and Document Services

In Lab 5, students use a member server to practice creating and configuring printers. Then, they use Group Policy to deploy a printer through Active Directory Domain Services, using the domain controller to confirm their success.

Table 5
Lab 5 Configuration Requirements

SVR-DC-A	SVR-MBR-B
Install Windows Server 2012	Install Windows Server 2012
Set Time Zone	Set Time Zone
Configure TCP/IP: IPv4 address: 10.0.0.1 Subnet Mask: 255.255.255.0 DNS Server 10.0.0.1	Configure TCP/IP: IPv4 address: 10.0.0.2 Subnet Mask: 255.255.255.0 DNS Server 10.0.0.1
Change Computer Name	Change Computer Name
Install the Active Directory Domain Services role	Join to adatum.com domain
Promote the server to a domain controller for adatum.com	
Turn on Network Discovery	

Lab 6. Configuring Servers for Remote Management

In Lab 6, the students use their servers to establish administrative connections in a variety of ways. This lab uses a standard three-server configuration that will be repeated in many of the labs upcoming in this manual.

Table 6
Lab 6 Configuration Requirements

SVR-DC-A	*SVR-MBR-B*	*SVR-MBR-C*
Install Windows Server 2012	Install Windows Server 2012	Install Windows Server 2012
Set Time Zone	Set Time Zone	Set Time Zone
Configure TCP/IP: IPv4 address: 10.0.0.1 Subnet Mask: 255.255.255.0 DNS Server 10.0.0.1	Configure TCP/IP: IPv4 address: 10.0.0.2 Subnet Mask: 255.255.255.0 DNS Server 10.0.0.1	Configure TCP/IP: IPv4 address: 10.0.0.3 Subnet Mask: 255.255.255.0 DNS Server 10.0.0.1
Change Computer Name	Change Computer Name	Change Computer Name
Install the Active Directory Domain Services role	Join to adatum.com domain	Join to adatum.com domain
Promote the server to a domain controller for adatum.com		

Lab 7. Creating and Configuring Virtual Machine Settings

In this lab, students practice creating and configuring virtual machines in a Hyper-V environment. This presents a problem when the lab environment itself relies on virtual machines.

When, as in the MLO environment, a lab server running Windows Server 2012 is itself a guest on a Hyper-V server, you can only install the Hyper-V role using the DISM.exe tool from the command line. This is because DISM.exe bypasses the normal prerequisites check. Also, although you can create virtual machines on a second generation Hyper-V server (that is, a guest Hyper-V server running on a host Hyper-V server), you cannot actually run them.

Lab 7 is designed so that the lab servers can run as guests on a Hyper-V host server. In a virtualized classroom environment, you can provide students with a Hyper-V server running three guest servers on virtual machines, and they will be able to complete the labs successfully. The labs have not been tested with any other hypervisor products.

Table 7
Lab 7 Configuration Requirements

SVR-DC-A	*SVR-MBR-B*	*SVR-MBR-C*
Install Windows Server 2012	Install Windows Server 2012	Install Windows Server 2012
Set Time Zone	Set Time Zone	Set Time Zone
Configure TCP/IP: IPv4 address: 10.0.0.1 Subnet Mask: 255.255.255.0 DNS Server 10.0.0.1	Configure TCP/IP: IPv4 address: 10.0.0.2 Subnet Mask: 255.255.255.0 DNS Server 10.0.0.1	Configure TCP/IP: IPv4 address: 10.0.0.3 Subnet Mask: 255.255.255.0 DNS Server 10.0.0.1
Change Computer Name	Change Computer Name	Change Computer Name
Install the Active Directory Domain Services role	Join to adatum.com domain	Join to adatum.com domain
Promote the server to a domain controller for adatum.com		

Lab 8. Creating and Configuring Virtual Machine Storage

In Lab 8, students continue their work with Hyper-V virtual machines and, in this case, their virtual storage capabilities. For this lab, the two member servers must have the Hyper-V role installed prior to the commencement of the lab. As in Lab 7, if you are working in a virtualized environment, you must install Hyper-V using the DISM.exe tool from the command prompt.

As with Lab 3 and Lab 4, this lab requires the SVR-MBR-C server to have three hard disks, in addition to the system disk. You must initialize the disks and create simple volumes on them before the commencement of the lab.

Table 8
Lab 8 Configuration Requirements

SVR-DC-A	SVR-MBR-B	SVR-MBR-C
Install Windows Server 2012	Install Windows Server 2012	Install Windows Server 2012
Set Time Zone	Set Time Zone	Set Time Zone
Configure TCP/IP: IPv4 address: 10.0.0.1 Subnet Mask: 255.255.255.0 DNS Server 10.0.0.1	Configure TCP/IP: IPv4 address: 10.0.0.2 Subnet Mask: 255.255.255.0 DNS Server 10.0.0.1	Configure TCP/IP: IPv4 address: 10.0.0.3 Subnet Mask: 255.255.255.0 DNS Server 10.0.0.1
Change Computer Name	Change Computer Name	Change Computer Name
Install the Active Directory Domain Services role	Join to adatum.com domain	Join to adatum.com domain
Promote the server to a domain controller for adatum.com	Install Hyper-V role using DISM.exe	Install Hyper-V role using DISM.exe
	Install Hyper-V Management Tools using Add Roles and Features Wizard	Install Hyper-V Management Tools using Add Roles and Features Wizard
		Initialize the three additional hard disks
		Create a simple volume on each of the three additional disks

Lab 9. Creating and Configuring Virtual Networks

In Lab 9, students complete their work with virtual machines by creating and configuring virtual switches. As in Lab 8, you must install Hyper-V on the SVR-MBR-C server prior to the commencement of the lab using DISM.exe.

Table 9

Lab 9 Configuration Requirements

SVR-DC-A	SVR-MBRB	SVR-MBR-C
Install Windows Server 2012	Install Windows Server 2012	Install Windows Server 2012
Set Time Zone	Set Time Zone	Set Time Zone
Configure TCP/IP: IPv4 address: 10.0.0.1 Subnet Mask: 255.255.255.0 DNS Server 10.0.0.1	Configure TCP/IP: IPv4 address: 10.0.0.2 Subnet Mask: 255.255.255.0 DNS Server 10.0.0.1	Configure TCP/IP: IPv4 address: 10.0.0.3 Subnet Mask: 255.255.255.0 DNS Server 10.0.0.1
Change Computer Name	Change Computer Name	Change Computer Name
Install the Active Directory Domain Services role	Join to adatum.com domain	Join to adatum.com domain
Promote the server to a domain controller for adatum.com		Install Hyper-V role using DISM.exe
		Install Hyper-V Management Tools using Add Roles and Features Wizard

Lab 10. Configuring IPv4 and IPv6 Addressing

In Lab 10, students calculate IP addresses and reconfigure their three servers with the new addresses. For this lab, it is essential that each group of three servers be connected to a network that is isolated from any other virtual machines or classroom computers.

Table 10

Lab 10 Configuration Requirements

SVR-DC-A	SVR-MBR-B	SVR-MBR-C
Install Windows Server 2012	Install Windows Server 2012	Install Windows Server 2012
Set Time Zone	Set Time Zone	Set Time Zone
Configure TCP/IP: IPv4 address: 10.0.0.1 Subnet Mask: 255.255.255.0 DNS Server 10.0.0.1	Configure TCP/IP: IPv4 address: 10.0.0.2 Subnet Mask: 255.255.255.0 DNS Server 10.0.0.1	Configure TCP/IP: IPv4 address: 10.0.0.3 Subnet Mask: 255.255.255.0 DNS Server 10.0.0.1
Change Computer Name	Change Computer Name	Change Computer Name
Install the Active Directory Domain Services role	Join to adatum.com domain	Join to adatum.com domain
Promote the server to a domain controller for adatum.com		

Lab 11. Deploying and Configuring the DHCP Service

In Lab 11, students deploy and configure the DHCP server service on SVR-DC-A. Because DHCP servers must have static IP address, you must configure the IPv6 address as well as the IPv4 address for this lab.

Table 11

Lab 11 Configuration Requirements

SVR-DC-A	SVR-MBR-B	SVR-MBR-C
Install Windows Server 2012	Install Windows Server 2012	Install Windows Server 2012
Set Time Zone	Set Time Zone	Set Time Zone
Configure TCP/IP: IPv4 address: 10.0.0.1 Subnet Mask: 255.255.255.0 DNS Server 10.0.0.1 IPv6 address: fd00::10:0:0:1	Configure TCP/IP: IPv4 address: 10.0.0.2 Subnet Mask: 255.255.255.0 DNS Server 10.0.0.1	Configure TCP/IP: IPv4 address: 10.0.0.3 Subnet Mask: 255.255.255.0 DNS Server 10.0.0.1
Change Computer Name	Change Computer Name	Change Computer Name
Install the Active Directory Domain Services role	Join to adatum.com domain	Join to adatum.com domain
Promote the server to a domain controller for adatum.com		

Lab 12. Deploying and Configuring the DNS Service

In Lab 12, students use the SVR-MBR-C server to remotely manage the DNS server running on SVR-DC-A.

Table 12

Lab 12 Configuration Requirements

SVR-DC-A	SVR-MBR-B	SVR-MBR-C
Install Windows Server 2012	Install Windows Server 2012	Install Windows Server 2012
Set Time Zone	Set Time Zone	Set Time Zone
Configure TCP/IP: IPv4 address: 10.0.0.1 Subnet Mask: 255.255.255.0 DNS Server 10.0.0.1	Configure TCP/IP: IPv4 address: 10.0.0.2 Subnet Mask: 255.255.255.0 DNS Server 10.0.0.1	Configure TCP/IP: IPv4 address: 10.0.0.3 Subnet Mask: 255.255.255.0 DNS Server 10.0.0.1
Change Computer Name	Change Computer Name	Change Computer Name
Install the Active Directory Domain Services role	Join to adatum.com domain	Join to adatum.com domain
Promote the server to a domain controller for adatum.com		

Lab 13. Installing Domain Controllers

Unlike most of the previous labs, Lab 13 must begin with all three computers configured as standalone servers. The students will, in the course of the lab, configure all three servers to function as domain controllers in various configurations.

Table 13
Lab 13 Configuration Requirements

SVR-DC-A	SVR-DC-B	SVR-DC-C
Install Windows Server 2012	Install Windows Server 2012	Install Windows Server 2012
Set Time Zone	Set Time Zone	Set Time Zone
Configure TCP/IP: IPv4 address: 10.0.0.1 Subnet Mask: 255.255.255.0 DNS Server 10.0.0.1	Configure TCP/IP: IPv4 address: 10.0.0.2 Subnet Mask: 255.255.255.0 DNS Server 10.0.0.1	Configure TCP/IP: IPv4 address: 10.0.0.3 Subnet Mask: 255.255.255.0 DNS Server 10.0.0.1
Change Computer Name	Change Computer Name	Change Computer Name

Lab 14. Creating and Managing Active Directory Users and Computers

In Lab 14, students practice creating Active Directory objects. In preparation for the lab, you must create an organizational unit called People in the adatum.com domain.

Table 14
Lab 14 Configuration Requirements

SVR-DC-A	SVR-MBR-B	SVR-MBR-C
Install Windows Server 2012	Install Windows Server 2012	Install Windows Server 2012
Set Time Zone	Set Time Zone	Set Time Zone
Configure TCP/IP: IPv4 address: 10.0.0.1 Subnet Mask: 255.255.255.0 DNS Server 10.0.0.1	Configure TCP/IP: IPv4 address: 10.0.0.2 Subnet Mask: 255.255.255.0 DNS Server 10.0.0.1	Configure TCP/IP: IPv4 address: 10.0.0.3 Subnet Mask: 255.255.255.0 DNS Server 10.0.0.1
Change Computer Name	Change Computer Name	Change Computer Name
Install the Active Directory Domain Services role	Join to adatum.com domain	Join to adatum.com domain
Promote the server to a domain controller for adatum.com		
Create an OU called People		

Lab 15. Creating and Managing Active Directory Groups and Organizational Units

In Lab 15, the students practice creating group and OU objects. No special preparation is required.

Table 15
Lab 15 Configuration Requirements

SVR-DC-A	SVR-MBR-B	SVR-MBR-C
Install Windows Server 2012	Install Windows Server 2012	Install Windows Server
Set Time Zone	Set Time Zone	Set Time Zone
Configure TCP/IP: IPv4 address: 10.0.0.1 Subnet Mask: 255.255.255.0 DNS Server 10.0.0.1	Configure TCP/IP: IPv4 address: 10.0.0.2 Subnet Mask: 255.255.255.0 DNS Server 10.0.0.1	Configure TCP/IP: IPv4 address: 10.0.0.3 Subnet Mask: 255.255.255.0 DNS Server 10.0.0.1
Change Computer Name	Change Computer Name	Change Computer Name
Install the Active Directory Domain Services role	Join to adatum.com domain	Join to adatum.com domain
Promote the server to a domain controller for adatum.com		

Lab 16. Creating Group Policy Objects

In Lab 16, students create Group Policy objects and link them to organizational units. To prepare the domain, you must create an OU and a group, and then add the SVR-MBR-C object to both, so that the server can receive the settings from the GPO the students create.

The students' final challenge in the lab is to demonstrate how the SVR-MBR-C computer has received the settings from the GPO. To do this, they must be aware that they can use the Resultant Set of Policy (RSOP) snap-in to view a computer's operative Group Policy settings. There is no indication of this in the lab manual, so the instructor should be prepared to give the students a hint, if necessary.

Table 16
Lab 16 Configuration Requirements

SVR-DC-A	SVR-MBR-B	SVR-MBR-C
Install Windows Server 2012	Install Windows Server 2012	Install Windows Server 2012
Set Time Zone	Set Time Zone	Set Time Zone
Configure TCP/IP: IPv4 address: 10.0.0.1 Subnet Mask: 255.255.255.0 DNS Server 10.0.0.1	Configure TCP/IP: IPv4 address: 10.0.0.2 Subnet Mask: 255.255.255.0 DNS Server 10.0.0.1	Configure TCP/IP: IPv4 address: 10.0.0.3 Subnet Mask: 255.255.255.0 DNS Server 10.0.0.1
Change Computer Name	Change Computer Name	Change Computer Name
Install the Active Directory Domain Services role	Join to adatum.com domain	Join to adatum.com domain
Promote the server to a domain controller for adatum.com	Disable Internet Explorer Enhanced Security Configuration	Disable Internet Explorer Enhanced Security Configuration
Create an OU called Paris		

Table 16
(*Continued*)

SVR-DC-A	SVR-MBR-B	SVR-MBR-C
Move the SVR-MBR-C computer object from the Computers container to the Paris OU		
Create a global group in the Users container called Servers		
Add the SVR-MBR-C computer to the Servers group		

Lab 17. Configuring Security Policies

The students, having installed Group Policy Management Tools in Lab 16, can begin Lab 17 with the tools already installed.

Table 17
Lab 17 Configuration Requirements

SVR-DC-A	SVR-MBR-B	SVR-MBR-C
Install Windows Server 2012	Install Windows Server 2012	Install Windows Server 2012
Set Time Zone	Set Time Zone	Set Time Zone
Configure TCP/IP: IPv4 address: 10.0.0.1 Subnet Mask: 255.255.255.0 DNS Server 10.0.0.1	Configure TCP/IP: IPv4 address: 10.0.0.2 Subnet Mask: 255.255.255.0 DNS Server 10.0.0.1	Configure TCP/IP: IPv4 address: 10.0.0.3 Subnet Mask: 255.255.255.0 DNS Server 10.0.0.1
Change Computer Name	Change Computer Name	Change Computer Name
Install the Active Directory Domain Services role	Join to adatum.com domain	Join to adatum.com domain
Promote the server to a domain controller for adatum.com	Install Group Policy Management Tools	

Lab 18. Configuring Application Restriction Policies

The students, having installed Group Policy Management Tools in Lab 16, can begin Lab 18 with the tools already installed.

Table 18
Lab 18 Configuration Requirements

SVR-DC-A	SVR-MBR-B	SVR-MBR-C
Install Windows Server 2012	Install Windows Server 2012	Install Windows Server 2012
Set Time Zone	Set Time Zone	Set Time Zone
Configure TCP/IP: IPv4 address: 10.0.0.1 Subnet Mask: 255.255.255.0 DNS Server 10.0.0.1	Configure TCP/IP: IPv4 address: 10.0.0.2 Subnet Mask: 255.255.255.0 DNS Server 10.0.0.1	Configure TCP/IP: IPv4 address: 10.0.0.3 Subnet Mask: 255.255.255.0 DNS Server 10.0.0.1
Change Computer Name	Change Computer Name	Change Computer Name
Install the Active Directory Domain Services role	Join to adatum.com domain	Join to adatum.com domain
Promote the server to a domain controller for adatum.com	Install Group Policy Management Tools	

Lab 19. Configuring Windows Firewall

In Lab 19, students use Windows Firewall to control access to a web server. To avoid interruptions and error messages, instructors should configure Internet Explorer and turn off Internet Explorer Enhanced Security Configuration before the students begin the lab.

Table 19
Lab 19 Configuration Requirements

SVR-DC-A	SVR-MBR-B	SVR-MBR-C
Install Windows Server 2012	Install Windows Server 2012	Install Windows Server 2012
Set Time Zone	Set Time Zone	Set Time Zone
Configure TCP/IP: IPv4 address: 10.0.0.1 Subnet Mask: 255.255.255.0 DNS Server 10.0.0.1	Configure TCP/IP: IPv4 address: 10.0.0.2 Subnet Mask: 255.255.255.0 DNS Server 10.0.0.1	Configure TCP/IP: IPv4 address: 10.0.0.3 Subnet Mask: 255.255.255.0 DNS Server 10.0.0.1
Change Computer Name	Change Computer Name	Change Computer Name
Install the Active Directory Domain Services role	Join to adatum.com domain	Join to the adatum.com domain
Promote the server to a domain controller for adatum.com	Disable Internet Explorer Enhanced Security Configuration	Disable Internet Explorer Enhanced Security Configuration
	Configure Internet Explorer with express settings	Configure Internet Explorer with express settings

CONFIGURING LAB SERVERS

For each of the tasks in the preceding tables, there is a set of instructions in the following sections. To configure the required environment for a particular lab, perform each of the specified tasks for each computer in the lab environment.

Installing Windows Server 2012

1. Insert the Windows Server 2012 installation disk. The Windows Setup page appears.

2. Click Next to accept the default values for the *Language to install, Time and currency format*, and *Keyboard or input method* parameters. Another Windows Setup page appears.

3. Click the *Install now* button. The *Select the operating system you want to install* page appears.

4. Select Windows Server 2012 Datacenter (Server with a GUI) and click Next. The License terms page appears.

5. Select I accept the license terms and click Next. The Which type of installation do you want? page appears.

6. Click Custom: Install Windows only (advanced). The Where do you want to install Windows? page appears.

7. Select Drive 0 Unallocated Space and click Next. The Installing Windows page appears as the system installs Windows Server 2012.

8. After several minutes and a system restart, the Settings page appears.

9. In the Password and Reenter password text boxes, type Pa$$w0rd and click Finish. The Windows security page appears, showing the time.

Configuring the Time Zone

1. Click the Server Manager icon on the Taskbar. The Server Manager console appears.

2. In the left pane, click Local Server. The Properties tile appears in the right pane.

3. Click the Time Zone value. The Date and Time dialog box appears.

4. Click Change Time Zone, if necessary. The Time Zone Settings dialog box appears.

5. In the Time Zone drop-down list, select the (UTC -05:00) Eastern Time (US & Canada) time zone and click OK.

6. Click OK to close the Date and Time dialog box.

Configuring the TCP/IP Client

1. Click the Server Manager icon on the Taskbar. The Server Manager console appears.

2. In the left pane, click Local Server. The Properties tile appears in the right pane.

3. Click the Ethernet value. The Network Connections dialog box appears.

4. Right-click the Ethernet connection and, from the context menu, select Properties. The Ethernet Properties sheet appears.

5. Double-click Internet Protocol Version 4 (TCP/IPv4). The Internet Protocol Version 4 (TCP/IPv4) Properties sheet appears.

6. Select the *Use the following IP address* option and type values in the following text boxes:
   - IP address
   - Subnet mask

7. Select the *Use the following DNS server addresses* option and type a value in the following text box:
   - Preferred DNS server

8. Click OK to close the Internet Protocol Version 4 (TCP/IPv4) Properties sheet.

9. If necessary, double-click Internet Protocol Version 6 (TCP/IPv6). The Internet Protocol Version 6 (TCP/IPv6) Properties sheet appears.

10. Select the *Use the following IPv6 address* option and type values in the following text boxes:
    - IPv6 address
    - Subnet prefix length

11. Select the *Use the following DNS server addresses* option and type a value in the following text box:
    - Preferred DNS server

12. Click OK to close the Internet Protocol Version 6 (TCP/IPv6) Properties sheet.

13. Click OK to close the Ethernet Properties sheet.

14. Close the Network Connections window.

Changing the Computer Name and Joining a Domain

1. Click the Server Manager icon on the Taskbar. The Server Manager console appears.

2. In the left pane, click Local Server. The Properties tile appears in the right pane.

3. In the Properties tile, click the *Computer name* value. The System Properties sheet appears.

4. Click Change. The Computer Name/Domain Changes dialog box appears.

5. In the Computer name text box, type the new name for the computer.

6. Select the Domain option and, in the Domain text box, type **adatum.com** and click OK. The Windows Security dialog box appears.

7. In the User name text box, type **Administrator**.

8. In the Password text box, type **Pa$$w0rd** and click OK. A Welcome to the adatum.com message box appears.

9. Click OK. A message box appears, prompting you to restart the computer.

10. Click OK.

11. Click Close to close the System Properties dialog box. Another message box appears, prompting you to restart the computer.

12. Click Restart now. The system restarts.

Enabling Network Discovery and File Sharing

1. Open the Windows Control Panel. The Control Panel window appears.

2. Click Network and Internet. The Network and Internet window appears.

3. Click Network and Sharing Center. The Network and Sharing Center window appears.

4. Click *Change advanced sharing settings*. The Advanced Sharing Settings dialog box appears.

5. In the currently active profile, select the Turn on network discovery and turn on file and printer sharing options.

6. Click Save Changes.

Installing the Hyper-V Role

1. Click the Windows PowerShell button on the Taskbar. An Administrator: Windows PowerShell window appears.

2. At the Windows PowerShell prompt, type the following command and press Enter:

   DISM /online /enable-feature /featurename:Microsoft-Hyper-V

3. The system installs the Hyper-V role and prompts you to restart the server.

4. Press Y. The system restarts.

5. Logon to the computer using the domain Administrator account and the password **Pa$$w0rd**. The Server Manager console appears.

6. In the Server Manager console, select Manage > Add Roles and Features. The Add Roles and Features wizard appears, displaying the *Before you begin* page.

7. Click Next. The *Select Installation Type* page appears.

8. Leave the *Role-based or feature-based installation* radio button selected and click Next. The *Select Destination Server* page appears.

9. Click Next to accept the default local server. The *Select Server Roles* page appears.

10. Click Next. The *Select features* page appears.

11. Expand Remote Server Administration Tools and Role Administration Tools and select the Hyper-V Management Tools checkbox.

12. Click Next. The Confirm installation selections page appears.

13. Click Install. The *Installation Progress* page appears as the wizard installs the Hyper-V role.

14. Click Close. The Add Roles and Features Wizard closes.

Initializing New Hard Disks

1. In Server Manager, click Tools > Computer Management. The Computer Management console appears.

2. In the left pane, click Disk Management. The Disk Management snap-in appears.

3. Right-click the tile for the new disk and, from the context menu, select Online.

4. Right-click the tile a second time and, from the context menu, select Initialize Disk. The Initialize Disk dialog box appears.

5. Select the GPT (GUID Partition Table) option and click OK. The disk status changes to Online.

6. Repeat steps 3 to 5 to initialize additional disks.

Creating Simple Volumes

1. In Server Manager, click Tools > Computer Management. The Computer Management console appears.

2. In the left pane, click Disk Management. The Disk Management snap-in appears.

3. Right-click the unallocated space on a disk and, from the context menu, select New Simple Volume. The New Simple Volume Wizard appears, displaying the Welcome page.

4. Click Next. The Specify Volume Size page appears.

5. In the Simple volume size in MB spin box, type the size of the volume you want to create and click Next. The Assign Drive Letter or Path page appears.

6. Click Next. The Format Partition page appears.

7. Click Next. The Completing the New Simple Volume Wizard page appears.

8. Click Finish. The wizard creates the volume, and it appears in the disk pane.

9. Repeat steps 3 to 8 to create additional volumes.

Disabling Internet Explorer Enhanced Security Configuration

1. Click the Server Manager icon on the Taskbar. The Server Manager console appears.

2. In the left pane, click Local Server. The Properties tile appears in the right pane.

3. In the Properties tile, click the IE Enhanced Security Configuration value. The Internet Explorer Enhanced Security Configuration dialog box appears.

4. Select the Off option for both Administrators and Users and click OK.

Installing Group Policy Management Tools

1. In Server Manager, click Manage > Add Roles and Features. The Add Roles and Features Wizard appears, displaying the Before you begin page.

2. Click Next. The Select installation type page appears.

3. Click Next. The Select destination server page appears.

4. Click Next. The Select server roles page appears.

5. Click Next. The Select features page appears.

6. Scroll down and select the Group Policy Management checkbox.

7. Click Next. The Confirm installation selections page appears.

8. Click Install. The Installation progress page appears as the wizard installs the selected features.

9. Click Close. The wizard closes.

Moving a Computer to an OU

1. On a domain controller, in Server Manager, click Tools > Active Directory Users and Computers. The Active Directory Users and Computers console appears.

2. Right-click the adatum.com domain and, from the context menu, select New > Organizational Unit. The New Object – Organizational Unit dialog box appears.

3. In the Name text box, type the name of the new OU and click OK. The system creates the new OU.

4. Select the Computers container. Right-click the computer object you want to move and, from the context menu, select Move. The Move dialog box appears.

5. Select the OU you created and click OK. The system moves the computer object to the OU.

Adding a Computer to a Group

1. On a domain controller, in Server Manager, click Tools > Active Directory Users and Computers. The Active Directory Users and Computers console appears.

2. Right-click a container or OU and, from the context menu, select New > Group. The New Object – Group dialog box appears.

3. In the Group Name text box, type the name of the new group and click OK. The system creates the new group.

4. Right-click the group you created and, from the context menu, select Properties. The group's Properties sheet appears.

5. Click the Members tab, and then click Add. The Select Users, Contacts, Computers, Service Accounts, or Groups dialog box appears.

6. Type the name of the computer you want to add in the Enter the object names to select box, and click OK.

7. Click OK to close the Properties sheet.

Configuring Internet Explorer with Express Settings

1. On the Start screen, click the Internet Explorer tile. The Internet Explorer window appears and displays a Set up Internet Explorer 10 screen.

2. Select the Use recommended security and compatibility settings option and click OK.

3. Close the Internet Explorer window.